ISBN-13: 978-0-9885855-1-5
BISAC CODE: BIO005000

TVGuestpert & TVGuestpert Publishing are visionary media companies that seek to educate, enlighten, and entertain the masses with the highest level of integrity. Our full service production company, publishing house, management, and media development firm promise to engage you creatively and honor you and ourselves, as well as the community, in order to bring about fulfillment and abundance both personally and professionally.

Nationwide Distribution through Ingram & New Leaf Distributing Company

Book Cover by Jonathan Fong
Author Headshot by Joe Buissink
Book Design by Lynette Ubel – Ubel Design
Edited by Jackson Truax, Jackie Petruzzelli and Stephanie Cobian

Published by TVGuestpert Publishing
11664 National Blvd, #345
Los Angeles, CA. 90064
310-584-1504
www.TVGPublishing.com

First Printing April 2015
Printed in the United States of America
10 9 8 7 6 5 4 3 2 1

JACK H. HARRIS

FATHER OF THE BLOB

The Making of a Monster Smash and Other Hollywood Tales

By Jack H. Harris

Dedication

For Judith,
Who came into my life to
teach me about really loving,
letting go, and allowing my
emotions to flow.

Acknowledgments

I am sadly the sole survivor of my original family of six, having lost my Mother early on and my three sisters to various forms of cancer: Mitzie at age fifty-six, Claire at age seventy-one, and Dotzie at eighty-one years of age. I mourn them sincerely.

Yet, I'm a perennial optimist. I never quit or became overwhelmed, tirelessly overcoming all obstacles. My crystal-clear memory has unobstructed speed in calling up past traumas and disappointments. There is joy and pride in my good fortune, to be part of the creative, demanding, frustrating and rewarding life of show biz. I enjoyed my ninety-sixth birthday, un-retired, in good health and sound mind. I continue daily, joined by my soul mate, Judith, to devote my time and attention to a life and a business that has rewarded me so handsomely.

One of my most important accomplishments was to father a worthy family dynasty. When I was forty-six, my darling daughter Lynda, the now famous POM Juice Queen, made me a grandfather. Her son, Jonathan, was joined by her son, Jason, two years later. My son, Anthony, a successful composer, author, and music conductor, and his dear wife, Alizon, presented me with two grandsons, Kris and Zach, and two gorgeous granddaughters, Jordanna and Gavrielle.

My guitar-playing grandson, Jason, fathered two adorable great-granddaughters, Danielle and Scarlett. Jason's sincere wish is to someday introduce me to his grandson.

Stewart Resnick, Lynda's second husband, added step-grandchildren, Jeffrey, Ilene and Bill. Ilene and hubby Daniel added a bright and beautiful step granddaughter, Lucy, and handsome step-grandson, Oliver, to the brood.

Not to understate my accomplishments, my lucky star led me to the relationship with my beautiful, witty, and intelligent mate-for-life, Judith Parker Harris, who happily fell into being a step-mom, step-grandma and step great-grandma when she married me.

We make a formidable group when we are together, especially at mealtimes. While my business relationships have always been built on loyalty and trust, business trust is intellectual. It comes from the brain. What Judy taught me, was how to trust the people I love with my heart. Judy, if you're reading this, I love you every day for it. I hope my family and friends know that you made me as successful in love and in life as I had been in pictures. To my Grandkids, to their Grandkids, and to everyone reading this, I hope you all meet (if you haven't already) someone who will love and change you in all of the ways that Judy has loved and changed me.

My sincere thanks to these people who chronologically affected my development:

Sarah Liebowitz Harris, Mom, gave me her engagement ring converted to a lion's head ring which never leaves my hand.

Ben Harris, Dad, taught me to do right by not emulating his way.

Shia Liebowitz, Gramps, introduced me to pomegranates from his fruit-peddling cart.

Jacob Harris, Gramps, blessed me with his name.

Bill Liebowitz, Uncle, gave me my first boy hair cut at age three.

Miss McCandless, my third grade teacher, enabled me to skip fourth grade.

Melvin Fox, theatre owner, appointed me manager of his new Mayfair Theatre, I was eighteen and he hounded me until I won a trip to Hollywood for my promotional stunts.

Pete Smith, self-appointed guide on my Hollywood trip, advisor for eventual permanent return to Hollywood.

David E. Millgram, theatre magnate, made me Publicity Manager for his twenty theatres.

Edna R. Carroll, awarded me the first PA censor Board approval for a sex movie.

Captain Arnold Patterson, recommended my transfer from combat field artillery to Officer Conversion School instructor in North Ireland.

General Bershon B. Sommerville, transferred me from the Officer Conversion School in Northern Ireland to U.S. Officer's Candidate School in New Jersey, U.S.A.

Lou Kellman, for partnering with me in a Philadelphia area distributing film exchange office.

Allan Freedman, N.Y. lab owner, who connected me to numerous film producers.

Irvine H. Millgate, for his original, *original* monster idea.

Irvin S. Yeaworth, for his excellent direction, THE BLOB, 4 D MAN and DINOSAURUS.

Jackson Truax, for his love of the movies and facile editing that always helped to pull out the story and cut the fluff.

Jacquie Jordan for believing in this book enough to expertly guide it through the publishing and promotion process – always patient, always there.

Brian Witten and Richard Saperstein, for their most thorough preparation of THE BLOB sequel.

Lynda "Pom Queen" Resnick, darling daughter and great supporter. Anthony R. Harris, swell son and marvelous music guide.

Judith P. Harris, great wife, without her no book, no star, no BLOB gaming machines.

Table of Contents

Introduction

For anyone reading this, I'd like to start by saying, "Thank you." I've been so incredibly fortunate to have had such a wonderful life and career in movies. While I owe so much of that to hard work, dedication, and everything I set out to learn and accomplish, ultimately it's the audience who decides if a film is successful or not. It's a strange tango. As filmmakers, it's our job to keep the audience entertained. If they deem us successful, we get to keep making movies.

I've gotten to keep making movies, mostly because of how much audiences loved and continue to love my signature film, THE BLOB. Whatever memorabilia remains from the 1958 film are rare collectables. There's now an annual BLOBFEST, and the film continues to entertain audiences throughout the world in theaters, TV, and in the various formats people are now watching movies on at home.

At the age of ninety-six, I decided to write a book about my life. Although I'm often asked to speak at BLOB-related events and to film students, it would be foolish of me to think I'll be able to do it forever. Now with this book in the world, fans of THE BLOB will always be able to learn something about how the film came to be made.

It's been a great pleasure to work with young filmmakers over the years. I've met talented and ambitious young people coming to America for the first time or having just graduated film school: people with names like John Carpenter, John Landis, or Ivan Reitman. If you're a young film student reading this, you might be the next name to join those influential and successful ranks; my sincerest wish is that you will be. Although I want this to be as entertaining a read as possible, I'll try and include some very tangible and very important life lessons about picking a project, finding the money, dealing with a dry spell, finding distribution, and benefitting from the fine points of a deal.

If you're reading this on the beach or on the way to your summer vacation, first off, consider me jealous. If you're a great fan of film history looking for a fun, casual afternoon of reading, I've included a lot of "Hollywood stories" from a life in which a kid from working-class Pennsylvania ended up living next to Barbra Streisand, vacationed with Frank Sinatra, and discovered Steve McQueen.

If you're one of my grandchildren or great-grandchildren reading this, hopefully you'll get all of that out of this book, and so much more. Most of my life was such incredibly hard work. Now I've found more joy than I could ever have dreamed possible, by preparing this book. Compiling the lessons and stories herein was a great undertaking for myself, with the help of my wonderful and supportive wife, Judith. It's been a long road from deciding to assemble this, for you now reading it. For my family, aspiring filmmakers, Hollywood enthusiasts, cinema aficionados, and BLOB fans alike, I hope you all have as much fun reading it as I had writing it.

Prologue

When Steve McQueen was hopelessly ill with Mesothelioma, a rare form of lung cancer, and hosting a huge tumor, he flew to Mexico to try Laetrile. Tragically, this was unsuccessful in arresting the disease. He had become a born again Christian, and he called Evangelist Billy Graham to come and pray with him. Billy was a close friend and mentor of "Shorty" Irvin S. Yeaworth, Jr., the President of Valley Forge Films Inc., who later directed THE BLOB. Billy told Shorty, who shared with me, that he entered the simple cabin where Steve was helplessly lying in bed. Billy looked around the room and saw blinds on the window, a cot, a couple of chairs, and a table. Steve died three days later, the only decoration on the wall, behind the bed, was a poster of THE BLOB. Steve's death shattered me. His performance in THE BLOB helped to change my life. I shall always remember the moments we shared and his BLOB poster legacy.

INDESCRIBABLE...
INDESTRUCTIBLE!
NOTHING CAN STOP IT!
THE BLOB
STEVEN McQUEEN
ANETA CORSEAUT · EARL ROWE
PRODUCED BY
JACK H. HARRIS
DIRECTED BY
IRVIN S. YEAWORTH, JR.
SCREENPLAY BY
THEODORE SIMONSON AND KATE PHILLIPS
FROM AN IDEA BY IRVINE H. MILLGATE
A TONYLYN PRODUCTION · COLOR BY DE LUXE

Chapter 1: The Blob

A few weeks after my initial brainstorming session with Irvine H. Millgate, producer/writer, concerning THE BLOB, I was in New York at the St. Regis Hotel for an early morning meeting the next day with my franchise holder in Manhattan. After a late dinner, I fell asleep about 11:30 PM when I was rudely awakened by the telephone at 2:30 AM. Who the hell would have the guts to call me at this hour?

I sleepily picked up the receiver and said, "Yes?"

From out of the earpiece burst the exclamation, "Jack! We've got it, I have the answer."

It was Irvine calling me from California.

He went on, "We have a monster never done before. It's a mineral form of life from another world. It defies gravity by climbing trees and has the ability to zap prey. It can fall from any height on to the ground and reform itself at the bottom."

I said, "Ok, is it a threat to mankind?"

"God damn right," Irvine replied. "It consumes flesh on contact."

"How's it destroyed?" I asked.

Irvine came right back with, "It's indestructible. It will resist fire, bullets, poison, acid…"

"How are we going to do it in?" was my next question.

Irvine said, "This is as far as I've gotten. I'm coming into New York tomorrow to have dinner with you so we can work out the details. Unless you think I'm on the wrong track."

By this time it was well past 3:00 AM. I was really taken with the idea and decided that we should meet at once and try to work it out. I went through my chores the following day and went back to the hotel to await Irvine's arrival.

We ordered dinner up in my suite and went to work. I questioned, "When it absorbs flesh, shouldn't it grow in size?"

Irvine answered, "Great!"

I asked, "How in the hell are we going to do this monster in?"

He showed me a bunch of schematic drawings showing how this stranger could slide up a wall and down the opposite side. Then, defy gravity by leaping upon its victims. It had to be able to withstand fire, gunfire, acid, and poison by just absorbing them and shrugging it off.

I said, "Well if we can't kill it, we'll have to immobilize it."

He exclaimed, "Right!"

We looked at each other and both said, "Freeze it." That would be our big surprise for the audience. We had the monster and the ending. It was a dynamite combination.

He said to me, "It has to have a name."

I said, "Lava – that's no good."

He said, "The Mineral Monster."

I said, "On a marquee that wouldn't draw flies."

We finally decided on a very classy working title, "The Molten Meteor," which I explained would have no chance of being on the finished movie.

Now we had a basic idea and a working title, but no story or plot line. We spent the following day together trying to come up with a storyline.

All we could put together was a series of horrifying incidents showing how voracious and terrifying the molten meteor could be. This wouldn't make a very good short subject.

Irvine asked me how I would finance the picture. I said that everything in my business life happened because I made it happen. As far as the financing goes, "I'll make that happen too."

He offered, "Let's try this on some money people and see how good it is."

I said, "This is very premature, but the idea of the unique monster is fascinating." I set a meeting the following week in New York, which we would both attend.

We met with Michael Friedman and Lou Kellman, my long time friend and the fellow that had introduced me to a Christian religious pictures studio in Chester Springs, Pennsylvania. Over lunch, Irvine and I described the uniqueness of the monster to include how to arrest it, and the horrific capabilities it had. Michael looked me in the eye and said, "Jack, you definitely have something here."

Lou looked at the floor, "Too gruesome! Count me out."

I said to Michael, "I have no idea what this will cost. I'll know in about a month, after I've had a chance to get a synopsis of a story put together. Then I'll noodle the production costs with some people in that specialty."

My next trip was a return to Chester Springs, PA with Millgate where we met with Irvin Shortess Yeaworth (he was 6' 3" and his friends at college nicknamed him "Shorty" and it stuck). Shorty had assembled a group of talented, anxious amateurs who were attracted to his cause of communicating the good word of the Bible through the medium of motion pictures. I already knew they had made about 400 of these Church films. He had writers, cameramen, grips, and electricians, and all of the personnel usually associated with filmmaking. Shorty became very enthusiastic when learning of our idea. He called their production manager, Russ Doughten, and their head writer, Ted Simonson, into the meeting.

The five of us kicked around ideas for character and story. Sadly, we didn't get very far.

A few days later we met in my film distribution office in Philadelphia on a quiet Saturday. I had Ed Prizer, my sales manager, at the meeting because he could type faster than any of our secretaries. I naively thought we could brainstorm an idea, and he could quickly record it. Five hours of this useless enterprise produced baskets of wastepaper.

Ted Simonson, the only real writer in the group said, "Mr. Harris."

I said, "That's my father's name, call me Jack."

Ted looked awe struck and hesitated to say, "Jack, I have an idea, but I'd like to work on it. Give me a few days and I'll come up with something."

Shorty looked pleased and surprised.

I said, "Ted, take your time, but hurry, and let's see what you come up with. One other thing you guys can do for me is to come up with an exciting name for the monster."

Shorty said, "If we ever make the picture, the cast and crew will come up with monickers and we'll have the name for the monster before it's finished."

Once things started to get serious, I set up a meeting with Shorty. Film production was new to me. Since I had little to no idea how to budget a movie, I needed the crew and equipment Shorty had assembled and his obvious enthusiasm to help get the movie made. Shorty had made no secret of his exclusive dedication to the creation of religious films. When I challenged his ability to devote himself to my monster movie, he told me of a meeting with his top staffers discussing the project. He was able to tell them, "The monster represents God's wrath at the failings of humanity."

To my knowledge, his devotion to religious films wasn't an issue with our subsequent films together. I don't know why and we never discussed it. Maybe he was taking the money he made from our movies and funding more religious pictures.

Irvine H. Millgate went back to New York, the film crew went back to Chester Springs. Ten anxious days went by while I awaited a storyline. All we had so far, which wasn't so bad, was a mineral form of life that consumed human flesh on contact and if not arrested or destroyed would envelop the earth. I took the concept to my banker, Lloyd Bechtel, who was the senior vice president of the 100 year old bank named The Pennsylvania Company. He looked at me with crazy eyes and told me that my history with the bank was excellent. If I wanted to borrow money I would have to present a business plan that made sense, but that the bank was not in the business of backing movies.

I understood that my relationship with The Pennsylvania Company for movie financing would be a small portion of the budget and strictly based upon my ability to repay the loan. I knew I had to go elsewhere.

I spoke to Ted Schlanger, President of Stanley/Warner Theatres, with a circuit of 200 movie palaces. He asked me a stupid question, "Suppose the movie dies at the box office?"

In all my years in the business, I never had a movie as certain to be valuable as THE MOLTEN METEOR could be, and I told him so.

He said he'd think about it. His company was capable of financing ten movies but wasn't in the business of doing so. Even though, without movies, there was little success to be had in owning theaters.

I went through a number of other potential investors and came up short. Though I was a most successful and experienced exhibitor and distributor, I had never made a movie before. Who the hell was I to be so audacious as to ask them to gamble on me?

Ted Simonson showed up with a very workable storyline where a group of teenagers encountered the molten meteor and through a series of misadventures were able to overcome the monster.

Every weekend for the next month was spent in story meetings at Chester Springs. To my great delight, we wound up with the almost ready script for our picture. Shorty wanted a professional touch, which I thoroughly agreed with, and he got his friend, Kate Phillips (her married name, she had also used Kay Linaker), to edit the script on spec. Kate was a staff writer for CBS and supposedly wrote a lot of their fiction stories. Shorty wanted her to add some New York-ese to the screenplay. The first thing she did when she showed up was insult Shorty's wife Jean, who said, "Get her out of here, or I'll start a war." After two days, in exchange for $125 and a writing credit, her services were terminated. That was the price Shorty paid for keeping peace with his wife. Phillips' name being on the poster and everything else was all a part of this deal with Shorty. She had nothing to do with the final film. The fact that she has taken credit for the film she didn't deserve and is erroneously credited in various places on the internet and elsewhere as having named the film is a very small yet very wet towel on the film and its legacy.

No thanks to Kate, we now had what literally became the shooting script we were looking for. It was 1953 and we were ready to find a financing partner.

I sent copies of the script to Disney, Paramount, 20th Century Fox, Warner Brothers and Universal Pictures, and wound up with a collection of very polite rejection letters. Nobody saw the merit in the project. I felt they were ridiculous, and they only increased my desire to get the picture made.

Now I set about budgeting the picture which I, in my conservative way, insisted would not exceed the sum of $100,000. 30% of which would go to the Valley Forge Film Group for their participation, leaving us with $70,000 for all other budget costs. I worked without compensation.

I was able to contribute $15,000 to the budget by taking a second mortgage on my home and borrowing what I could from the bank. I went to Michael Friedman with a budget and plan, and he got his brother, Allan, then President of DeLuxe Laboratories, to come up with about $25,000 worth of necessary lab work for the picture, also part of the budget. Michael and I agreed to be equal partners on the film if he would also come up with the missing $60,000, and guarantee any over budget costs.

If and when the picture was sold, Irvine and I would share a credit for the original idea and also split a $5,000 fee for coming up with it. We were ready to make a movie.

Now we were facing a new terror – casting.

We had a screenplay and the money in place, so we started pre-production, and early on realized that the teenage protagonist would have the major burden of making this monster come to life. We lined up all the special effects, both animation and miniatures, but had to find our male lead.

One Saturday night I was watching "Playhouse 90" on TV with my son. He started yawning and excused himself. My wife, Muriel also took a pass, but I was interested in a young William Shatner and a middle-aged Ralph Bellamy, as father and son lawyers defending a suspected murderer.

The father and son entered the holding cell where an interesting looking teenage delivery boy was silently fretting his fate. He was suspected of murdering one of the female customers of the market where he worked. As the father and son fenced back and forth about the defense, the delivery boy just sat and fumed.

The case started building, and in the last few minutes of this ninety-minute show, the delivery boy electrified me with a sudden outburst of "How can you defend me, if you act like you don't even know I'm here in the room with you? I didn't do it, and if you don't believe me, you shouldn't be here."

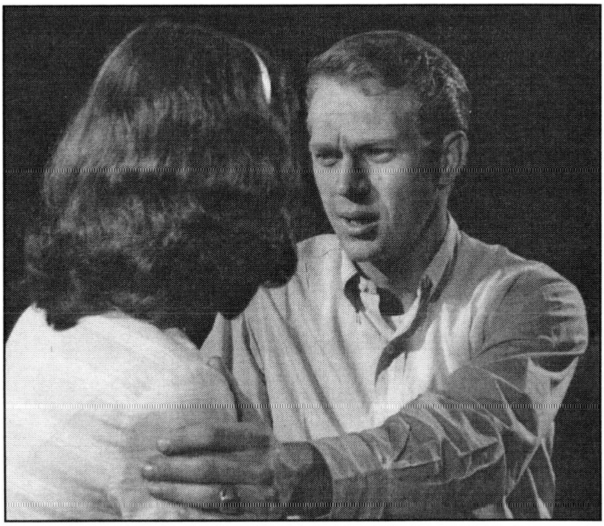

Steve McQueen, star of THE BLOB, was discovered by Jack H. Harris while performing in the Broadway show, Hat Full of Rain, 1954.

I was deeply affected by his performance, and found his name to be Steve McQueen. I immediately called Shorty and told him of my excitement, and he said, "We know him. He's a dirty guy, a trouble maker and a nuisance."

I asked, "How?" It turns out that Steve was then married to Neile Adams, a Broadway and Hollywood musical star who had worked on a three-day shoot for a Valley Forge Films religious film the previous summer. Steve hung around the production and made everybody glad to see the rear license plate of his car as he and Neile exited at the conclusion of production.

Two days later, I was invited by my friend, Ben Schrift, a New York banker and uncle of Shelly Schrift (Shelly Winters), to see her new play, "Hat Full of Rain," on Broadway. Ben Gazarra was her co-star and I was anxious to see the play.

That night, before the curtain rose, a cast change was announced. Ben Gazarra was ill, and his part would be played by Steve McQueen, his understudy.

I was enthralled by the production and by Steve's performance, but held my comments about a movie until I could sit down with my production partners. After much haggling, I pulled my rank and said, "It's my idea. I'm the producer. I financed it. I want Steve McQueen to be our star. I want you guys to use your past relationship with him to strike a guild minimum deal."

Shorty Yeaworth and Russ Doughten, our production manager, spent two hours with Steve and his manager, Hilly Elkins, softening them up for my appearance to clinch the deal, which I did. I was deeply impressed by Steve and his manager, and their favorable reaction to our screenplay.

Now for the rest of the cast: They were mostly selected from the small group of teenagers then performing in live theatre in New York. One would recommend another and since we already had Steve, his three buddies in the movie; Tony, Mooch and Al were pretty easy to cast. Earl Rowe, famous for his national food commercials, made a great head cop.

Irvin S. (Shorty) Yeaworth (Left) directs THE BLOB as Producer, Jack H. Harris (2nd from the left) and the crew look on.

I remembered Olin Howland from his teacher role in the David O. Selznick movie, TOM SAWYER. He nailed the part of the old man who first discovers the Monster's meteorite.

Next we had to find our leading lady. We had been through fifty auditions without results when a new Broadway actress named Aneta Corseaut was brought to our attention. We had two actresses ready to sign, but they weren't right. Aneta took the Pennsylvania railroad train in New York one morning and met us at the Penn Station in Philadelphia. We spent two hours with her at the station. She did a test scene for us and really came to life when she read from the screenplay.

We signed her at once, which was a good thing, as we were scheduled to commence shooting three days later. She went on to establish herself in television and is best remembered as Andy Giffith's main squeeze in "The Andy Griffith Show."

Hedgerow, "the Actor's Studio of Philadelphia," was the source of our casting for the other parts in THE MOLTEN METEOR.

We had a five-week shooting schedule of six twenty-hour days a week. It was grueling. Steve lived up to his billing. He was more difficult than any major superstar could ever be.

Early in the shooting schedule when I was in my Philadelphia office, I got an emergency, telephone call from Russ Doughten. "Jack, ya' gotta come out here right away." It was a one-hour drive. "Steve has been busted and is being held in the police station for reckless driving. We think it would make a big impression on McQueen if you showed up and got him released. Everybody is on schedule and cannot leave the set."

I jumped in my car and almost risked being cited for speeding. I got to the police station and bailed out Steve and his dog, Wolf, a big, black, ferocious looking German Shepard mix who was his constant companion off the set. I told Steve he could continue on the picture but would be grounded from using his souped-up MG Sports Roadster during the shooting schedule. The roads in and around the shooting area were narrow, twisty and winding. If they were negotiated at more than twenty-five miles per hour, the car was a dangerous projectile. Steve easily doubled that limit. When caught by the cops, he averaged fifty miles per hour.

I calmly explained to Steve that he was the star of the production, and we were on a vicious shooting schedule to make sure we didn't run out of money and not be able to pay our bills. He was sympathetic and agreeable and only snuck his car into the roads two more times that we know of. At least he wasn't caught again by police, or worse killed.

Although this was his second movie, McQueen had about a fifteen-minute part in SOMEBODY UP THERE LIKES ME, starring Paul Newman. Steve conducted himself like a true star. He was disagreeable, haughty, charming, standoffish, chummy, and crazy making, yet endearing.

Viewing his later efforts, I believe there's no argument that he achieved great stardom. In later years when I talked to Harold Hecht about the making of THE GREAT ESCAPE, he told me, "He was a pain in the ass, and I'll never work with him again – until I need him."

Shorty had a policy of not inviting the actors to the dailies screenings. The dailies were quick prints of all of the day's takes from the previous day. He felt the actors would watch their scenes then start emoting their ideas of what was called for in the show. During one day's shooting, about the second week, I get a call from Hilly Elkins demanding that Steve be invited to the dailies screenings. I rushed to the set and during a break in the action, took Steve and Shorty into the office and watched a battle royale being played out between Shorty, asserting his directorial prerogative, and Steve, demanding his star input.

I listened and compromised by ordering the director to invite Steve to the screening of every third day's shooting. For the record, Steve was a no-show at about half of the screenings he was invited to attend, but never stopped bitching about the whole idea of not having actors at the screenings. When he did attend, he was mostly silent.

We had elected to produce one of the most difficult types of movies known – a literate, sensible monster movie that had to impact the audience and also receive kindness from the critics. We should have had quadruple the budget to use, but we didn't. We had to make up for it with spit, grit, and muscle, plus clear thinking.

At the start of production, we still had only "THE MOLTEN METEOR" as a title. It was Shorty's opinion that somewhere in the trims and outtakes somebody would call the monster a usable name. We examined every inch of work picture and found nothing.

As production proceeded, everyone in the cast and crew was invited to put their ideas for a title on a large black board. One name I recall was THE GLOB THAT GIRDLED THE GLOBE.

We were getting ready to shoot main titles and still had no finished title. By vote we decided to call it, THE GLOB. I was leaving the location just after approving the title cards, and about three miles from the studio, I was stopped by a motorcycle cop on my way back to Philadelphia, saying, "There's a dire emergency and you must get right back to Chester Springs."

Siren wailing, I arrived in minutes. Shorty greeted me at the gate with, "We applied for a copyright on the title, THE GLOB and found it had already been awarded to Walt Kelly and his syndicated comic strip."

I was already running late for my Philadelphia meeting. I hurriedly said, "Let's see. We have a title, THE GLOB, on a title card and ready to shoot. A-L-O-B – that doesn't spell anything. B-L-O-B – that spells BLOB – that's our title, THE BLOB." We only had to change one letter. We knew that was great for the budget and the picture. It was a most fortuitous ten minutes.

How do you create a Blob? We had to have substance that would pour down a wall and reform itself on the floor below, leaving no trace of itself on the wall. That meant it couldn't be too loose. It also had to have girth for the reformation on the floor to have some dimensionality. We tried a number of substances and wound up with a clear, silicone material.

Now, for giving it color. We tried all then known dyes, paints, and pigments and were fortunate enough to interest 3M in solving our problem. They came up with a special dye compound, which mixed with the silicone and penetrated it thoroughly. The result was a red, gelatinous mass.

We had a member of the crew standing by, because the one difficulty was that the dye, if left standing, would separate itself from the silicone into a separate puddle. As long as the mixture was kept whipped up, the color was consistent. This was accomplished in a special drum labeled, "THE BLOB – DO NOT TOUCH." The crewmember, Whipper, was known as the "Wrangler of The Blob."

There's a scene in THE BLOB where the kids are looking to warn people and see if they can find any trace of the monster. They approach a huge bush in the park, and the leaves suddenly start to rustle. The kids part the branches and are embarrassed to break up two young lovers make-out session. The girl was Pamela Curran, a famous model and fiancé of Tom McDermott, the then-reigning tennis great, who was also heir to a fortune. After the picture was completed, she invited me to a cocktail party at her New York penthouse. She introduced me all around as the producer of her latest movie. People were filing out and she asked me to stay behind, which I did. In a few minutes, the doorbell rang, and there was this handsome, hair-slicked-down, dressed in black-tie, young fellow standing at the door. They apparently had never met before. At that time, he was an actor at 20th Century Fox who had been sent to escort her to a premiere of a movie, and she proudly introduced me as, Jack H. Harris, the producer of her latest movie.

He said to me, in a voice lower than mine (and mine's famous for being low) "Hello, Mr. Harris, it's so nice to meet you. I'm Bob Evans, and I know our paths will cross in the future." Evans ultimately became head of Paramount, and made it the most successful studio in Hollywood by greenlighting THE ODD COUPLE, ROSEMARY'S BABY, LOVE STORY, and THE GODFATHER, among others.

I saw the two of them off in a waiting taxi as I went back to my hotel.

When THE BLOB was in rough-cut and going through four months of special effects and opticals, I pressed the staff accountant into an accurate prediction of how many dollars this was going to eventually cost. His best number, in cutting all corners, was $30,000 over budget, a total of $130,000.

I talked it over with Michael Freidman, and we both knew that Shorty had nowhere to get the $30,000. This meant his penalty was to lose his 25% profit participation. Shorty was thrilled to make this arrangement, as were we. Michael agreed to put up the extra $30,000.

The wrap party for completion of THE BLOB was held at my home in Penn Valley, Pennsylvania that consisted of a 4,000 square foot house with a swimming pool and a surrounding acre of highly cultivated plant materials. The cast and crew attended, with Steve McQueen making an extra effort to join the party.

He called me aside and said, "Jack, if I had any idea how great this movie would be, I would have held out for a percentage of the action."

THE BLOB turned out to be an enjoyable, somewhat scary, great word-of-mouth movie. I was sneak-previewing the picture, trying to get a feel for how I would premiere it and position it in the marketplace. At this point in time, it never occurred to me that I would not personally distribute the picture. After all, why should I throw away my twenty years of experience in the movie business? The only problem was at that time I took a look at the cost of launching the film in the way that I wanted to in order for it to be a great success. It was in the millions, which I didn't have.

One of the people invited to a sneak preview was Howard Minsky, who was the Eastern Division district manager for Paramount Pictures. He fell in love with the movie. He said, "You've got a good movie. Let me show it to my home office brass and see if we can strike a deal that will make you happy."

He took two weeks, screened the picture privately for the personnel concerned, and expressed his failure to develop their interest.

I took his idea and started screening the picture for the major studios and was winding up with a similar result. After about two months of an increasingly failing screening phase, I figured "Okay, they turned it down. To hell with them. I'll open it in one theater. I'll see what happens." Then I got a phone call from George Weltner, then President of Paramount Pictures. He said, "I don't know why they screened THE BLOB for everybody but me. We'll send a messenger over to pick up your print so I can look at the picture tomorrow."

I didn't argue with him. I got the print ready for his messenger. The print was in his hands that night. 11:00 AM the next day, he called me with an offer. He wanted to distribute the picture for seven years, throughout the world, theatrical only, paying me $300,000.

I figured if that was all I was going to get out of it, the picture had cost $130,000, that was a pretty good profit. That also meant that I would still get the picture back at the end of seven years. The only ancillary use of a movie at that point in time was television. In 1957, the televising of movies was between slim and none. I offered Weltner the TV rights for an additional $100,000. He took a day to think it over and he said, "Jack, I think you're stuck with the television rights." Which, as it turned out, was one of the greatest things I could have ever been stuck with. Only giving Weltner the rights for seven years, after which they reverted back to me, was the smartest thing I ever did. I knew that part of the business.

It was now time to sit down with Michael Friedman, and figure out how to divvy up the $170,000 proceeds. He wanted interest on his money, which I was also entitled to on my share. He deducted potential income taxes. I said, "Look, give me my money back, and $50,000 for my creation of this movie, in addition to the exclusive ownership of the copyright and the negative. You keep the rest." Apparently, I knew something he didn't know – the only thing positive is the negative. We shook hands on the deal.

Late in 1957, I got a phone call from actor/director, Dick Powell, who had become the head honcho at 4 Star Television. They were getting ready to do a series about a quick-triggered bounty hunter, called "Wanted Dead or Alive." He had seen scenes from THE BLOB, and the company was interested in working with Steve McQueen. They wanted to know if they should tangle with his now infamous temperament.

I said, "Dick, he's a temperamental jerk, but he's worth it. Your series will be graced by Steve McQueen." Steve got the job and the rest is history.

The Paramount deal was concluded in late 1957. The world premiere was held in California on Labor Day weekend, 1958. In the intervening year, my time was spent designing the advertising and publicity campaign along with the genius of Paramount's Publicity Director, Jerry Pickman.

Sidney Herman, one of Paramount's Vice Presidents, had been calling me to take a meeting so he could tell me his wonderful idea to put a new title song on THE BLOB. I found time for him and learned that he had negotiated a deal to license "Purple People Eater" as our title song. I was horrified.

I explained that the original music we had created and incorporated into the picture was completely synchronized with the title segues and the water ripple background to become more and more suspenseful and frightening. When the last title card came up, "THE BLOB," the timpani had the rhythm of a beating heart, and THE BLOB lettering flickered from black to bright red letters. Those who saw it were scared before the movie started.

Sidney was a bright, enthusiastic gentleman. A nice, little guy, and one of the hats he wore at Paramount was heading their music company. We talked a while, and I expressed my true feelings. He said, "You know, you're right. If we're going to do something, let's do something original. To hell with 'The Purple People Eater.'"

I didn't want anything original. I was pretty thrilled with what we had. Yet I felt that it couldn't hurt to see what he could come up with.

He had just signed a team made up of experienced composer, Mack David, and his sidekick, Burt Bacharach. Within a week, I was sitting with him, and the two songwriters who played their new Blob theme for me. It just hit me and I spontaneously said, "Let's go with it." "It" sold over three million copies and was free radio advertisement for the picture every time the title song was played, which was frequently.

Shorty vehemently disagreed with my decision and recounted for me the laborious hours it took to put together what we had. Why would I risk losing the mood that the main title section had created?

Now my exhibitor side came out and I replied, "Shorty, this is a fun movie, and a catchy title song will do it no harm."

A couple of months before the premiere, I found out that Paramount had sunk almost half a million dollars into a minor little black and white production called, I MARRIED A MONSTER FROM OUTER

SPACE. THE BLOB had been purchased as a second feature to their loser production. Though I wasn't too happy about it, I just knew that THE BLOB would find its way out of second place because it was head, shoulders, and feet above I MARRIED A MONSTER FROM OUTER SPACE.

When the double feature opened in about thirty selected theatres throughout the U.S., two of them did not receive the I MARRIED A MONSTER FROM OUTER SPACE prints. The results were enormous, and the best grosses came from the two houses that ran THE BLOB alone. This created a new model. THE BLOB suddenly became the top feature, and all promotion was devoted to THE BLOB.

It opened in territory after territory in the domestic United States. In that era, national theatre breaks were reserved for top, double-A features. After the California result, 300 theatres nationally opened the picture. Reading that week's *Variety* (the movie trade paper bible), grosses were so high, you'd think I had made them up myself. When opening the two pages that showed every territory and what their gross was, every single one of them said, *THE BLOB Wows Them In Philly, THE BLOB Breaks Records in Chicago, THE BLOB out grosses everything in Hartford, Boston, Detroit, Denver.* It was unanimous. THE BLOB was a hit, destined to become a sci-fi cult classic and acclaimed motion picture.

It didn't hurt us that Steve Allen, Jack Benny, Bob Hope, Burns and Allen, and most of the leading television talk show hosts of the day mentioned THE BLOB title whenever they needed a breakout laugh from the audience. This all translated into a golden flow of revenue at the theatre box offices.

Let it also be noted that like many of the films mentioned here, THE BLOB also had time to become a success. In this day and age, due to the ticket price and the overwhelming cost of distributing a film, the nature of this and the business have changed. The audience has a different view of going to the movies. I feel bad that I can't go today because of my hearing loss, but I watch all the DVDs that have captions.

Back at the multiplex, a movie can open and gross fifty million dollars its opening weekend. Then it can drop 60% the second week. There are exceptions, as some films do hold up for four or five weeks. Though now that's very rare. There's something wrong with that. It's a big country. There are plenty of ticker buyers. If a movie doesn't hit the first weekend it comes out, it loses screens. There simply aren't enough fascinating movies made to hold screens.

Despite movie studios putting tens of millions of dollars into their marketing campaigns, it's hard not to feel like these days opening a movie and sustaining any sort of success is always fighting an uphill battle in a way that we didn't face fifty or sixty years ago. The trailers and the ads haven't changed. The audience has changed. There's an argument that people would rather watch things on a laptop or TV at home, and not leave the house to drive somewhere or be a part of a communal experience.

Yet, there are still events that can pull communities out to the theatre, like BLOBFEST. Held annually at the theater where we shot the iconic scenes at The Colonial Theater in Phoenixville, Pennsylvania, BLOBFEST sells more tickets every year.

Even the BLOBFEST imitators in other theaters around the country make money. Much like my early theatre exhibition campaigns, these offered a sense of community, participation, and a quality of uniqueness pertaining to the film itself. Maybe social media marketing is providing some of that. Maybe that human touch of my old campaigns is lost and gone forever. Increasingly, so much distribution and exhibition is being taken over by such large chains, with little community input or involvement, if any. I don't know if a return to the kinds of promotions I used to do could turn around the attendance slump movie theaters are currently experiencing, but it's one of the biggest changes, and something I certainly miss.

One of my great thrills was standing at the corner of 44th and Broadway and looking across the street at the Astor Theatre marquee that announced THE BLOB as its New York premiere exclusive showing. This fulfilled a prophecy I had made to my dad years before to have a Harris Production on a marquee on Broadway. THE BLOB landed in the Variety Magazine Top 100 list, grossing over $5,000,000 in 1958.

THE BLOB continued to do great business in theatres in the UK, Germany, Italy and other parts of the international territory. After about eight months, my friends at Paramount returned to me the rights for Japan, Greece, and France. Japan had a serious quota system against foreign imports. France opened the picture with subtitles for a seven day showing in a Paris art house and bombed. Greece couldn't afford to import the picture. So there I was with three foreign territories to fill.

Early in 1962, I made a deal with Allied Artists Pictures (where I had been sales manager of the Philadelphia Distribution branch) to distribute THE BLOB in Japan to great business. In 1964, I licensed Sedimo, a Swedish company, to distribute THE BLOB in France and Greece to similar success. Paramount had given me an early return of the rights to THE BLOB, enabling me to give the theatrical reissue rights to Allied Artists for the USA.

One of the great post-script stories about THE BLOB and its legacy is being the first starring vehicle for Steve McQueen. Over the course of the next decade, Steve would go on to become one of the most popular movie stars in the world, starring in THE GREAT ESCAPE and BULLITT. He received an Oscar nomination for Best Actor in a Leading Role in 1967 for THE SAND PEBBLES, which is considered to be his finest dramatic work. It was around the time THE SAND PEBBLES was released that the rights for THE BLOB reverted from Paramount back to me. By the time I released the film again, unlike in the film's initial theatrical run, he received top billing. It was due, in large part, to Steve's work in the intervening years that THE BLOB has been such a continual success.

⌘

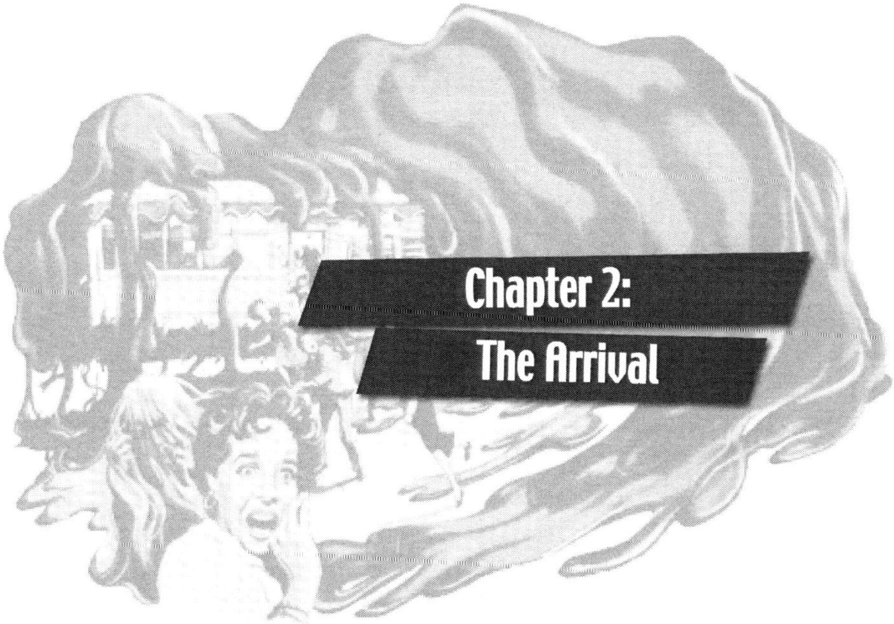

Chapter 2: The Arrival

The success of my future film career was defined by my immigrant roots. So before we get to Vaudeville or Hollywood, I'd like to begin with the story of my Grandparents. One thing that unites so many of us as Americans is that many of our families have an Ellis Island story. Here's how my Grandparents came to America and became the Harris Family over a century ago.

On June 1st, 1900, my Mother Sara Bessie (Saura Bassa) Liebowitz was born in Bucharest, Romania to proud parents John (Shia) and Anna (Chona) Liebowitz (Leibovich). John was a captain in the Romanian Army, assigned to look after the decoration details at the Royal Palace because of his artistic and sculpting skills. My Grandfather supervised and participated in the constant palace refurbishment.

My Grandmother Anna had spent her late teens in a very fashionable shoe store where handsome John swept her off her feet with a marriage proposal. Local caterer, Great Grandma "Bubba" Rose (Raizel) Fishman, Anna's mother, didn't fully approve of the union, so she kept a watchful eye on the proceedings. She welcomed Sara into the family with love and a possessiveness that John wished could also have been bestowed upon him.

Romania's then ruler King Carol I, called by his wife, Queen Elizabeth, "the monarch who even sleeps in his crown," reigned over his country with high standards of morality. It was also a time of anti-Semitism in Russia and Poland. The Queen advised Captain John to gather his family to head for America and saw to it that they had an easy immigration. Sara, at six months, traveled with her parents and her Bubba Rose to the USA in December, 1900.

In 1907, eleven-year-old Benny (Baerel) Ostravsky, who would grow up to become my Father, had to quit his successful job assisting the local blacksmith to join his mother Annie, four brothers, and three sisters in fleeing The Pogroms of Warsaw, then part of Russia. They had just enough money to travel steerage on a ship bound for New Jersey, USA. Two years earlier, Jacob Ostravsky, the family patriarch and an expert tailor, had gone ahead to London to work with a family that was established there. He then saw an opportunity to emigrate further to Philadelphia, Pennsylvania to establish a tailor shop so he could support his wife and eight kids. Like many immigrants of that time, his last name was changed at Ellis Island, in this case, from Ostravsky to Harris. The family was reunited in the city of brotherly love in the fall of that year. The tailoring success of Jacob (now Harris) continued, and one of his A-list clients was Buffalo Bill of circus fame.

Back on my Mother's side of the family, the Liebowitz clan had established an apartment above their shoe store in South Philadelphia. Anna was in her element. She was a successful businesswoman and mother, birthing two more girls and a boy. The business was thriving. The kids fostered rich lives for themselves and pride as Americans. Great Grandma Bubba Rose resumed her catering business, serving Romanian pastries for local ethnic restaurants.

John had a tougher time getting established. His was not the temperament for shoe store operation, and his baroque picture frames (his specialty) were not in style anymore in the United States. He assisted in construction and picture work, but couldn't shake his "Captain John" identity from the Old Country.

In 1905, the "flickers", early productions of the Thomas Edison invention of motion pictures, had spread across the USA. These short silent films were a revelation to the masses delivering new experiences to fans when shown in converted storefront halls. The movies ran from two to fifteen minutes each and consisted of westerns, romance, comedy, travel, and photographic tricks. Each ticket cost five cents, hence moviehouses being called "Nickelodeons." But by 1915, they had started to lose their appeal. That's when the smaller venues started shuttering and disappearing.

The larger auditoriums added four to six Vaudeville acts and sparked a new interest. Patrons paid their nickel and watched the unique live acts, then thirty-minutes of short films known as "chasers" were shown. Afterwards, theater staff would empty the house so that the bench seats would be available for the next live show, which ran five times a day.

By the time he was fifteen, Benny (now Harris) lost his father Jacob and two of his brothers. His distraught mother attended three funerals in nine months. His remaining older brother, Meyer, had taken over the tailor shop and married. Younger brothers Manuel and Abraham were in grammar school. His older sister, Jennie, worked in the tailor shop, the two youngest ones, Esther and Sarah, were in school. Benny was thrilled that being in America meant that he didn't have to work in a blacksmith shop anymore. Nevertheless, with the four younger siblings in school, he had to go back to work. The best paying job he could readily find was with a street repair crew for the trolley line.

Benny was working on a street one afternoon in North Philadelphia, and saw a sign advertising a "Nickelodeon." Benny asked a fellow workman what it was. The workman explained, "Oh, it's one of those nickel joints." This piqued Benny's interest, and his excitement increased with each word of explanation about the live show and the movies for five cents. At the end of his shift, Benny ran over to the theatre and plunked down his nickel. When he got inside the last act was finishing. The theatre went dark and the movies started with a Charlie Chaplin ten-minute silent short subject. He had never seen a film before.

Though not many people had either at this time. The cinematic art form, which would come to dominate the world's stage in the following decades, was still in its earliest days of Charlie Chaplin and Buster Keaton, only a few years removed from THE GREAT TRAIN ROBBERY and Georges Melies' immortal A TRIP TO THE MOON.

Entranced, Benny looked around and saw the light source for the show coming from a type of porthole at the back of the theatre. He went back there and climbed the wall ladder to the loft where the projector and projectionist were running the show. Benny asked the projectionist if he could watch him, and he kindly agreed. He then set up the next twenty-minute reel on the projector and proceeded to sit down and read a book. Afterwards, Benny asked him a lot of questions and the projectionist said, "Look kid, do you want a job? I need a helper."

Benny couldn't believe his good fortune. He took the job immediately, which almost doubled the pay he received on the road gang. His job was to rewind the film onto the reels at the end of each performance and then to put them in racks so that the full reels would be ready for the next showing. Then at the end of each three-day run, he carted two fifty-pound metal film cases via trolley car to the Vine Street film row where all of the Philadelphia film distribution offices were located. It was a dream job for the road gang worker. The night shipper would receive the film and have the next day's film ready for pick-up. Benny then took a reverse trolley ride and delivered them to the theatre.

About two years later, the night shipper at one of the film exchanges, Masterpiece Film, asked Benny if he was interested in a shipping and inspection job, which meant no more hauling of film back and forth. He said, "Yes" before the question was even finished. He spent two years as night shipper, before being promoted to day shipping supervisor overseeing ten ladies who inspected the films and two assistant shippers. That was Benny's introduction to film distribution, film repair, and film operation. The company was making major studio income. Movies were changing over from the Nickelodeon model eventually evolving into "features" running from thirty to eighty minutes. This was done as a way of developing starring roles for audience favorite players. Though this was met with some controversy within the industry, as some studio heads feared that using specific stars to sell films would lead to the stars asking for more money. Regardless, the business was changing, and Benny had gotten there at the right time. He worked as day shipping supervisor for about a year. Then he was promoted into the booking department. After a number of years went by, Benny was promoted again and became the assistant to the booker.

In the spring of 1916, Benny found himself unexpectedly smitten. He was on the street front of the two story Masterpiece Film Attractions building taking a break from the shipping room. Since he didn't smoke, he was enjoying the sunshine when his attention was drawn by girlie chatter. He gazed upon two attractive young ladies strolling down the street. He thought one of them was quite beautiful and he approached her to let her know. The girls stopped and giggled as Benny struggled for words.

He blurted, "I'm Benny Harris, what are your names?"

The amused girls volunteered, "Sara and Lucy." He would come to learn they were on a break from their jobs bottling sodas. They had been walking down Vine Street, taking in the window movie displays at the various distribution offices. Benny, being naturally knowledgeable about the latest films, shared the latest scoop on each one. They were especially impressed with Masterpiece Film. Benny's need to return to the shipping room ended his break, hoping he would see Sara soon.

Late in 1915, Sara's mother, Annie Liebowitz, had contracted the influenza that was epidemic across the United States and Europe. She died at the end of 1915. Her widower, John, was completely befuddled by the shoe store business and lost it within six months of her passing. His spotty income left him unable to provide for his children. He became a pushcart produce peddler and wound up as a boarder with his disdainful mother-in-law, Bubba Rose. Though Sara had a job at the soda bottling plant, her siblings, Eleanor, Bertha, and Samuel, were still little kids. Unable to work themselves, they tragically wound up in the Romanian Workman's Orphanage. Sara roomed with her dad and grandma until she could find a place of her own.

Meanwhile Sara's courtship with Benny had lasted about six months. Sara was just shy of five feet tall, with Benny an inch taller than her. He knew they made a cute little couple. Benny thought meeting this beautiful petite soda girl was the most remarkable happening in his newly adopted country. He couldn't wait to ask her to marry him. Sara, also smitten, couldn't help but reflect on her plight. She also figured that this marriage would assist in getting her siblings out of the orphanage. Her enthusiastic "Yes" sealed the merger.

Benny said, "There's one thing I have to do before we can get married: Get my mother's permission."

Although Sara was taken aback, she went along to meet Annie (coincidentally the same first name as her deceased mother) Harris. She looked over Benny's choice of a wife and said, "Well, he gives me $10 a week now. You can get married if he continues to give me $10 a week." Despite her anger at the suggestion, Sara kept her cool and agreed.

Sara and Benny were married in June of 1917. The United States had entered the World War I conflagration and it affected everybody. Benny's marital status exempted him from being called up to service. On Thanksgiving Day 1918, they welcomed their first born, me, Jacob Hershel Harris, into the world. The young parents were seventeen (Sara) and nineteen (Benny).

Ben and Sara Harris, Jack's parents, married June, 1917.

I was born at 2111 N. 29th Street, in a tiny one bedroom flat above a tobacco store. My parents had named me after my paternal grandfather. Sara, very superstitious, swore never to go to a hospital and die like her mother had, opting to birth me at home. Benny worked extra jobs and saved whatever money he could. By the time Sara was almost ready to deliver her second child, Claire, he was able to put a down payment on a three bedroom, one bath plus an outhouse home at 2119 N. 28th Street, only one block away.

"Strawberry Mansion" was a section of north Philadelphia, Pennsylvania adjoining Fairmount Park, a green paradise that could be traversed for fourteen miles in any direction without entering city streets. My family's row house was five city-blocks from the "Park" at 33rd Street.

Though my Father's career and business dealings continued to prosper, whatever love he had for his family he showered upon my sister. I was pained by this as a child but figured that I had my Mother. But I was only two years old. What did I know?

In 1921, at the tender age of three, I was being baby sat by my Uncle Bill (Samuel), aged thirteen, and his fifteen-year-old sister, my Aunt Bertie. They were both now out of the orphanage and living with Bubba Rose. We were sitting on the floor playing jacks when my uncle said, "I'm going to do it."

My Aunt Bertie replied, "You better wait 'til Sara gets home."

Uncle Bill said, "Jackie, how would you like to look handsome?"

It seemed a good idea to me, I agreed.

In a flash, Uncle Bill wielded scissors and a comb into my Jackie Coogan inspired Dutch bob. (All the rage in those days were in tribute to the Charlie Chaplin-Jackie Coogan classic, THE KID.)

I sat there quizzically and innocently, not worrying about a thing. I saw the hair falling on my face and my clothes and wondered what this hair cutting would prove. First thing I noticed was that without the hair covering my ears, I could hear better. When my Aunt Bertie carefully wiped the hair cuttings from my eyes, my vision was perfect. No more bangs.

Uncle Bill said to Aunt Bertie, "What do you think?"

She snapped back, "Sara will kill us."

He said, "I know what's missing. We have to have some pomade." He came back from the bathroom with a jar of Vaseline, which he proceeded to rub into my hair. Then he combed it back with a part on the left side. I heard a noise from Aunt Bertie. She was crying. Uncle Bill brought me a mirror. I was afraid to look into it. Until I realized, I kind of liked the '20s gigolo look. Uncle Bill said, "Son of the Sheik."

Almost at that point my Mother walked in, smiling as she looked around. Then, she saw me, and let out a wailing, "Oh no! What did you do to my Jackie? You ruined him. He looks terrible."

I figured my Mother must be right. But, I was confused. I thought I looked pretty good.

"Now he looks like a regular kid. If Rudolph Valentino ever had a son, he'd look like Jackie," Uncle Bill said, "Call him Jack." Turns out my Mother liked the look (and name) so much that she bought a jar of real pomade and put it on my hair after each wash.

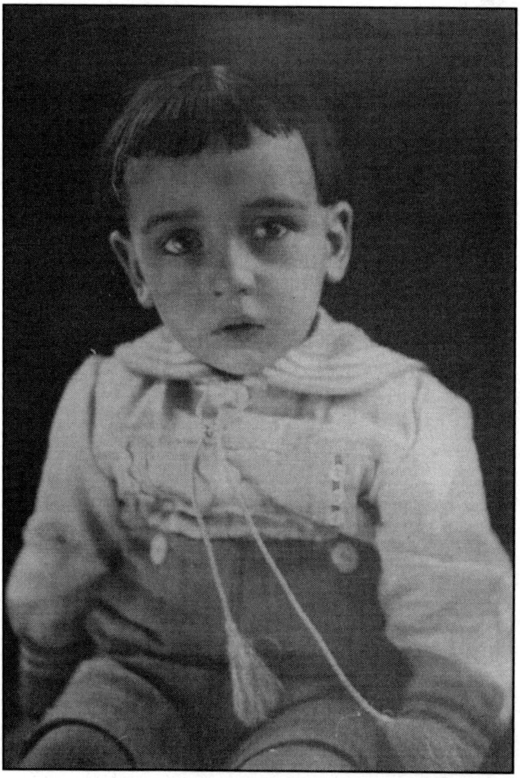

When my Father came home at dinnertime, my Mother had me wait in the kitchen and then asked my Father in and said, "Benny, notice anything different about Jack?"

My Father came in and threw his arms around me and mumbled something about, "He could be in the movies."

3-year-old Jack H. Harris after his first boy's haircut, courtesy of his Uncle Bill, 1921.

My Father would regale me with stories of his days running films as an assistant projectionist in a Nickelodeon Theatre, which was a storefront converted to an entertainment house by virtue of a series of raw, wooden benches spaced at intervals across the floor.

My Father had purchased a pair of cumbersome 35mm projectors, which I watched him grease, oil, and service every Sunday afternoon. He used these machines for private party showings which became his mainstay on evenings and weekends. I remember one Saturday afternoon when he said, "Go out and collect some of your pals and invite them over for a show." Each house in our row had a 12x14 foot backyard surrounded by a seven foot wood fence. I helped my Father hang a bed sheet on the inside wall of our fence. We then gathered our neighbors for the show. At dusk, a silent showing started with an OUT OF THE INKWELL cartoon, and an OUR GANG short followed by a Tom Mix western. At the end of the show, the applause of only twenty fans was so enthusiastic that it was deafening. It was 1923, and I already solidified my connection with the movies.

I remember one night when I was about five-years-old, we had a special dinner, home-cooked by my mom. As the dinner was starting, my Mother announced that this meal was to celebrate my Father's promotion to film booker. This meant that he was now a front office executive. My Mother and Father were non-smokers and tea drinkers, but there was a glass of wine at the table on this particular evening of which even I had a sip.

My Mother and Father were avid movie fans, and he thrilled at the metamorphosis of the movies. It was the best we had in those days. There was no television. There were live performances in Vaudeville and on Broadway, but gradually the movies came into their own and the theatres became quite numerous with plush seating from the wooden benches, and the projection systems grew slicker, with live organ and maybe piano musical accompaniment specifically tailored to the show.

One lazy Sunday when I was about seven-years-old, my Father was busy cleaning and lubricating his two sidejob 35mm silent projectors in the living room. My Mother was in the kitchen preparing our Sunday meal. My sister, Claire, was playing upstairs when the doorbell rang. I opened the door and was greeted by a very tall, ponderously plump, overdressed lady who asked for Benny Harris. I motioned inside and said, "He's right in there."

She offered me her hand and said, "You must be Jackie." I limply shook her hand and before I could ask, she told me, "I'm Alice Alexia Carton, assistant to your Father's boss, Mr. Korson." She brushed past me and entered the living room with "Hi ya, Benny! I was in the neighborhood and thought I'd stop by and say hello. Looks like you're busy so I won't stay long."

My Father parked his tools and wiped his hands. My Mother came quickly from the kitchen. They both made Miss Carton respectfully welcome. The three of them sat and talked, as I went to practice my ball throwing in the backyard.

After a short while my Mother called me, "Jackie, come in for a minute please."

I walked into the living room to see my Mother and Father visibly awed by Alice Alexia as they awaited my presence. "Go and ask him, Ben," said Miss Carton. My Father stood up and called me closer, "Jackie, what are you?" I unhesitatingly replied, "A boy."

Alice Alexia quickly interrupted with, "What is your religion?"

I thought for a moment, here we were in an all – Catholic, sixty-row house street. I'd often visited the Most Precious Blood Church with my neighbor buddies and even knew the head priest, Father Green. I knew the Holy Days – Ash Wednesday, Good Friday, and Palm Sunday. "Catholic," I blurted out, to my parents amazement and shame.

"See, Benny, I was right. You've got to get your kids a religious education," said Miss Carton.

My embarrassed Father turned to me with, "You're Jewish. You eat matzo on Passover, and you don't believe in Jesus."

Alice Alexia laughingly restrained him with, "Benny, now that you're aware of the problem, please don't try to resolve it in five minutes. He's a little boy, but a smart one. He'll get it, if you teach him."

My speechless Mother was quietly teary. My Father promised to follow through and thanked her. "Jackie, thank Miss Carton."

I walked over to her and said, "Thank you, Miss Carton." She leaned over, smothered me with a hug and a kiss, and put a quarter in my hand, saying, "You're a handsome, smart, young man. I'm sure you will quickly learn about God and religion. Bless you." She bade my folk's good day and was off in a flash.

When she was gone my Father asked me, "What religion are you?"

"Jewish," I quickly replied. That began my indoctrination by two non-practicing Jewish parents. They soon joined a Conservative Jewish Synagogue and re-learned, along with me, the history of the Jewish faith.

⌘

Chapter 3: The Performer

My Father made sure that I saw all of the important movies released from 1924 to 1936, for which I am eternally grateful. Along the way, I was bitten by the acting bug.

"Dancing lessons!" decreed my Mother. She was a beauty with a marvelous singing voice. Sadly, she also had what must be the world's biggest inferiority complex. She could enthrall the family with wonderful a cappella renderings, but wouldn't utter a note in front of strangers. When she enrolled my sister Claire in dancing school, I think her frustrated desire to be on the stage was her real motivation.

When it came to dancing, I thought Claire was the real talent. I enjoyed sitting and watching her. When we were in dancing school, and no one was watching, I would go into the next room, which was all mirrors. I played around with some Apache numbers that I had learned just by watching. The dancing teacher discovered me. She said, "Where did you take those lessons?" I said, "I watched my sister." The teacher said, "We've got a dance team here."

Vaudeville embraces dancing duo Jack and sister, Claire, 1925.

After six months of training, the teacher encouraged us to tour all of the nearby vaudeville venues on amateur night. This led to making a few appearances with major kiddie reviews. Five-and-a-half-year-old Claire was a French vamp with a slit skirt and saucy beret who was attracted to a slightly older gigolo (me at age seven) with slicked down black hair, long sideburns, black corduroy slacks and black silk t-shirt puffing on a fake cigarette. Our act began when she elbowed me in the back and knocked the cigarette out of my mouth. This was followed by us performing a precise execution of the then popular Apache dance. I would wink at the audience and they would all laugh. From our first time onstage, I knew that through entertainment and showbusiness I had found a new way to communicate with people.

We won first prize at numerous shows, appearing against competitors of all ages. What I liked best about the whole experience was taking a bow. In those days when you were performing in amateur night, the audience would throw money on the stage. My sister and I became very adept at finishing our dance and quickly cleaning up all the tossed money before we left the stage. We would then quickly deliver the money to our Mother. We went from picking up coins to eventually being paid to do our act. I loved touring as child Vaudeville performers. In addition to my connection with the audience and my time onstage, I fell in love with the magic and animal acts and learned many of their tricks. It was, what one might call, a "sweet gig."

Mom was our manager, caretaker, and mother. In addition to caring for Claire and me, as performers as well as children, she had given birth to twin girls, Mitzie and Dotzie, a year before our tour started. The strain of traveling around on boats and trains was increasingly difficult for her; it was hard to make the round trips and still be there in the morning to make sure everything went well with the infants. After almost a year into the tour, it was regretfully decided that we would retire from the stage for the good of the family.

One of our performances was seen by a talent scout who booked us into a movie production being shot on location in Conshohocken, Pennsylvania, about thirty miles from Philadelphia. It was being produced by a company that worked with Universal Studios. This location was chosen for filming post World War I Moscow because of a bunch of the broken down lots that already existed in the local area. My sister and I played street urchins begging for pennies in the film. I was in the background, leading the kids in some dancing. The film was on a two-week shooting schedule. I recall getting a fresh $5 bill each day as the company bus would pick us up in front of our home for the round trip to the location. My Father collected the money each evening.

During the shooting, I saw the production crew running around and doing their job, with the director executing his very full schedule. I noticed one man always well-dressed, wearing a derby, coming in and sitting in his chair next to the camera. Everyone was obediant to this gentleman. I asked the director who this important man was.

He said with gravity, "That's Mr. Weill, the producer."

I took careful note.

Almost one year later, I was sitting in a theatre in Atlantic City with my cousin, Bob. The trailers were on the screen. I was talking to a friend next to me and my cousin said, "Jack, Jack – that's you!" I had made it into the trailer. I was very proud. I don't recall ever having seen the completed film, ABIE'S IRISH BRIDE.

One night my Father arrived in a taxi with two men whom he had invited to dinner at our modest home. The older gentleman guest was first introduced to me as Boris Thomashefsky. Mr. Thomashefsky introduced the other guest, who was his nephew, Muni Weisenfreund. They were both in town having just completed an engagement at the Arch Street Theatre, also known as the Yiddish Arts Theatre, where Yiddish plays would try out before braving the theatres of New York City. Mr. Thomashefsky served as the theater's Managing Director.

My Mother had sent my three sisters to dinner with our aunt, and prepared a Romanian Jewish meal with all the trimmings, which was consumed with enjoyment of every morsel. The dinner started with momaliga (corn mush) appetizer followed by potlajela (eggplant) salad. The entrée was brustflanken, better known as beef breast sauté. For dessert, she prepared one of her famous dishes, pineapple upside down cake, which was consumed with tall glasses of Swee-Touch-Nee Tea. The twenty one-year-old nephew was leaving the following week for California, where he had a six-month contract with Warner Brothers to appear in their movies. I was awestruck to meet the great Thomashefsky and was pleased for, and a little envious of, his nephew who later would change his name to Paul Muni. It blazed across the screens of the world in films like I AM A FUGITIVE FROM A CHAIN GANG, THE LIFE OF EMILE ZOLA, THE GOOD EARTH, and one of his greatest roles, SCARFACE (1932). He made many films and was nominated four times for an Academy Award for Best Actor in a Leading Role, winning in 1937 for THE STORY OF LOUIS PASTEUR.

I was about eight years old when my Father was approached by one of his exhibitor clients to help him find someone to lease his theatre that was having tough times. After a few days, my Father decided to take his distribution knowledge and experience and apply them to running a theatre. He could keep his day job since the theatre ran matinees only on Saturday and Sunday. The theatre was called "The Gem." Situated on the border of tough Irish-American and African-American neighborhoods, we had a broad spectrum of potential clients. There was a house next door to the theatre that our family inhabited, which also made for a cozy arrangement. My Mother was cashier, my Father was manager, with one paid employee, the projectionist.

I became a star at school when the other kids discovered my family ran The Gem. It was fun to select friends to be my guest for Saturday Matinees. I assisted in distributing weekly programs to the homes in the area. Movies were still silent and we were last in the city to play a film. I recall a tenor who enlivened Monday nights with an in house live, vocal performance for a piece of the gross. We rigged up a speaker and were one of the first theaters to project a newsreel in sound. Alas, after a year, our limited finances ran dry. We gave up exhibition and moved back to the old neighborhood.

In 1928, a New York company decided to do a series of short kiddie films designed to compete with Hal Roach and his OUR GANG comedies. At the age of ten, I was booked into a three-day shooting schedule, with most of the action taking place at the Shibe Park Phillies Ball Club Headquarters. On the second day, during a shooting break, we kids went out to the baseball diamond to play. This was before Little League days. We drew lots of attention, and I was first up to bat. The pitcher pitched me a fastball and I connected with it and sent it to the outfield. I was so surprised. I just stood there when I heard this gravel voice behind me say, "Run you little son of a bitch, run." Which I did, and I got a homer. I was then introduced to my insistent coach, legendary ball player, Ty Cobb.

We finished the two-reeler, but it didn't take off. Once again, I never saw the finished product, though I loved the experience, especially seeing how movies are manufactured.

⌘

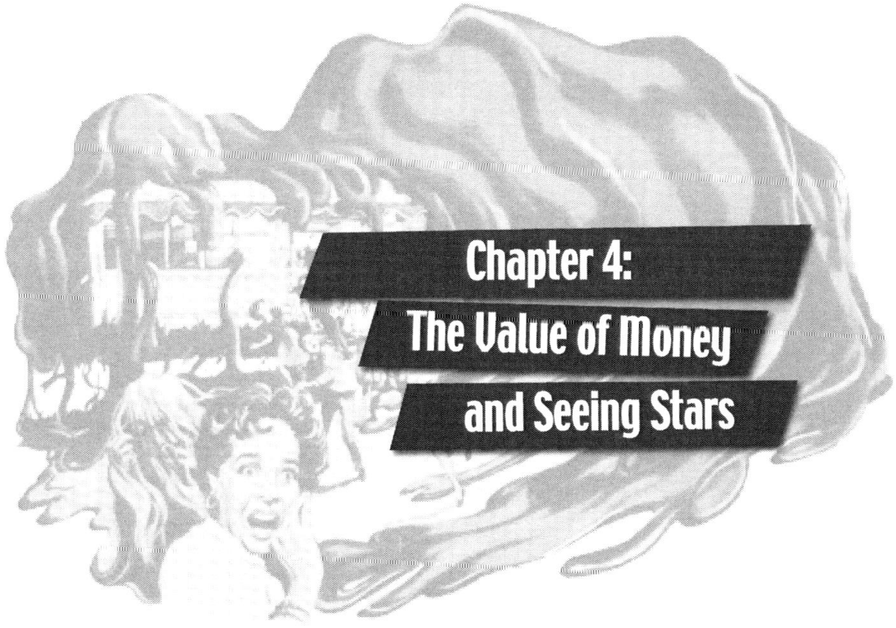

Chapter 4: The Value of Money and Seeing Stars

I was feeling unwell one day at school when my teacher sent me home early to see a doctor. My Mother took a look at her home-early-from-school son and put me right to bed. Getting in bed made me feel worse. I had joined the ranks of kids that contracted one of the most communicable diseases of the time, Scarlet Fever.

In those days, the city transported the victims to the Communicable Disease Hospital for a thirty-to-sixty day stay for treatment and cure. After almost four weeks of going through the evolving stages of recovery, I felt pretty good. I awaited my discharge examination, only to be told by the doctor that I couldn't leave the hospital until the skin peelings between my toes had stopped. I also examined my toes, and he was right.

I scored some apple butter and found the peeling responded temporarily to its application. The next exit exam found me furiously cleaning and reapplying the apple butter to my toes. I was ready for the doctor. When he examined me, I quickly closed my toes after each peek, and I passed.

The next day I was home bragging to my three sisters about my hospital stay. We had a great reunion of movies, a party, and a rapt audience for my adventures.

Four days later, my three sisters, Claire, Mitzie, and Dotzie all came down with a fever which became Scarlet Fever. The ambulance came for them and I was forced to return to the hospital as well. Apparently, I left the hospital three weeks too early. You can't cheat recovering from a serious ailment.

I made numerous trips through the years to visit my Father at The Film Exchange where he worked. It was usually an important occasion for my participation. I met many silent stars who would come to Philadelphia as one of their touring destinations when launching a new film nationally. Among these luminaries was William S. Hart, the famous cowboy star, Francis X. Bushman, the Harrison Ford of his day, and other screen stalwarts that gave me an inside look at this developing industry.

When the movies found their voice, I was as blown away as a ten-year-old could be. I went with my great-grandmother to see the movie that started it all, THE JAZZ SINGER. I was thrilled to hear Al Jolson talk and sing from the screen. My darling Bubba was practically stone deaf, though I can still see her smiling face when I watched her enjoying my enjoyment. She was happy to share this experience with me. We both talked a long time over glasses of tea and homemade cakes that she had personally baked. This new method of sound projection sounded the death knell of Vaudeville as we knew it. Movies didn't replace Broadway as a venue for new plays and musical reviews, but it certainly made the average vaudevillian look to other performance opportunities as the Vaudeville shows ceased, except for a few theatres in major cities.

One day, Bubba Rose took me to Atlantic City, about a two-hour bus trip from Philadelphia. She had a cane and a large shoulder bag. I helped her into two seats. I sat in front of her and we communicated over my shoulder. She frequently tugged my arm, and each time filled my hand with snacks. We got there and she sat on a bench on the boardwalk and we made a deal. I could go down on the beach provided we could see each other. I kept the bargain even when I walked into the sea.

A day on the Boardwalk of sightseeing and a chauffeured wheelchair ride ended with our stop at the bus terminal for our trip home. Even though she had plied me with never-ending treats, I wasn't prepared for the complete baked chicken and soda-pop she miraculously produced from her bottomless shoulder bag. After wolfing everything down, I caught a good nap before arriving in Philadelphia. I became the most intense ambassador for Atlantic City our family ever experienced.

My schooling continued and so did summer breaks. We prepared early. The whole family would spend a day in late April visiting Atlantic City to select an apartment near the sand where we could spend a two-week vacation in July. Every summer, my Mother would pack two steamer trunks, which were picked up by the New Jersey Messenger Service, a company devoted to physically moving film from the Philadelphia film exchanges to various theatres in New Jersey, and then returning them to their Philadelphia offices. The trunks were delivered to our selected Atlantic City address on July 10th, one day before our arrival. I recall a good night's sleep before each trip being impossible due to the anticipation. We went by automobile, chauffeured by one of my Father's friends since we had no car. I recall fondly those Atlantic City vacations. My Mother loved them because all six of us ate every meal at restaurants. We learned to swim in the ocean, and saw every movie in the various theatres. Life couldn't get any better. The Atlantic City vacations stopped when I was about fifteen. Later, I would go to the shore with friends as a young adult.

In 1932, the depression had our country in a stranglehold. Fortunately, my Father was in the right business at the right time and was able to support a wife and four kids due to his hard work in the movie business and my Mother's economies. My parents decided when I was twelve that it was time to have me tutored in being enabled to read the Yiddish newspaper and the Hebrew Holy Book, the Torah.

My Father said, "You're going to be Bar Mitzvahed."

I said, "What's that?"

Rabbi Hillel, former head of a tormented yeshiva in Russia, had immigrated to Philadelphia and was soliciting students to reestablish himself. He was a handsome, silver-maned stern tutor, who spoke Yiddish with a Russian accent. This conflicted with the way my Romanian family taught me to speak the mother tongue. But it saved me the time of traveling to a learning institution and gave me a one-on-one opportunity to prepare for my Bar Mitzvah.

My Father hadn't paid much attention.

One day I said to him, "Tell me about your Bar Mitzvah."

He said, "You're going to be angry."

I asked, "Why?"

He said, "I didn't get Bar Mitzvahed."

I asked, "What happened? Were you sick?"

He said, "No, I was playing with the boys. I hit a ball out so straight and nice. It was a home run. The boys gave me a gold cross as a gift. I went home and took my shirt off, and my Father saw the cross. My Father said to me, 'What's that cross?'"

He told his Father what it was that he was wearing.

His Father said, "Does that mean that you're a Christian?"

My Father had responded to him, "I don't think so. I think it just means that I'm an American. We're in America."

So his Father took the cross, and made 100 crosses on his back with it. He told him never to wear the cross again.

I asked him more, "What about your Bar Mitzvah?"

My Father explained to me that his Bar Mitzvah came, and his Father said, "You're going to get Bar Mitzvahed."

He responded to his dad, "I'm not going to get Bar Mitzvahed. Because I've got 100 crosses on my back, and I'd be thrown out of the synagogue."

So my Father didn't get Bar Mitzvahed.

As I approached my 13th birthday, thanks to Rabbi Hillel, I became adept at written Yiddish and Hebrew and actually looked forward to my ceremony with great confidence. It was a formal affair in two parts. The religious portion took place at a Saturday morning temple service. I had memorized my Torah "reading," and without looking at the scroll, proudly delivered the Hebrew words directly to the congregation to "Oohs and Aahs" from those assembled. When I had finished, everyone came rushing at me with five and ten dollar bills.

A black-tie dinner for eighty-five people at Uhrs Romanian Restaurant took place Sunday night. Various friends, family and business members said a few words at the podium. Then the Bar Mitzvah boy was called upon to speak. My show biz background helped me to deliver a ten-minute speech, first in English, then in Yiddish. I brought the house down. I was thrilled.

A five-piece band started to play as the Emcee started to announced, "Come on everybody, the music has started. Everybody dance – and if you can't dance you can 'hutska.'"

Actually, a Bar Mitzvah is 80% for the proud parents and 20% for the boy. My Father had arranged to have the entire ceremony filmed in 16mm and shown that same night after a break in the dancing. The guests applauded my dad for this unusual party touch. My Mother and Father reveled in it.

Many gifts were bestowed upon me that night, including watches, fountain pens, cuff links, gift certificates and money.

My Father asked, "How much money did you collect?"

I proudly replied, "$195.00" (pretty good in 1932).

"Good," he said. "We'll open your first savings account at the Pennsylvania Company." Even though the account was opened in his name and trust for me, I was flushed with joy. The bank passbook confirmed that I had taken my first serious step in acquiring money.

After my time spent working in Vaudeville and as a child actor, and before I started working for my Father as a projectionist, I had wanted to find other ways to make money. I think I was eight or nine when I realized that in those days not everybody had a telephone. There was a cigar store on the corner with four pay phones. I used to hang around there and deliver messages for nickels, which I kept in my pocket. Then I developed an ice route. I had a draw wagon. I used to go to the ice house and pick up pieces of ice. The pieces were five, ten, and twenty-five cents. I used to get a dime profit per piece. I learned early on to save that money.

Months went by as I saved what I had earned. My savings totaled the magnificent sum of $20.00. I told my Father I wanted to deposit it into my savings account. He produced my passbook and suggested that I personally make out the deposit. I was thrilled to make my first bank trip and handed my $20 and the passbook to the teller. She took the money and put the book into the comptometer, then handed it to me pointing at the record of the deposit. I checked it and noticed a mistake. The total was $30.00, a $185 difference from what it should have been. The teller checked and verified the difference was due to a withdrawal of that amount by Ben Harris.

That night at dinner I told my Father about what the bank said. He took me away from the dinner table into the next room so that we could talk privately.

"Look Jackie," he said, "The twins needed new school outfits. Since I was short, I knew you wouldn't mind if I borrowed it from you."

I felt hit hard, but held back the tears, "Dad, that's my money," I said, "and I wanted to keep adding to it."

My Father angrily said, "Your Bar Mitzvah cost plenty. You should appreciate how hard it was for me to pay the bills."

My Mother was shaken to learn that my account had been the money source for the twin's school outfits.

I inquired, "When are you going to pay me back?"

He said, "I knew you'd say that to me. That's the lousiest thing a son can say to a father."

I said "Okay."

My Father had the habit of borrowing money from family and friends who had the onerous task of trying to get repaid. Some never did. Conversely, regardless of his usual dire financial straits, he kept his home overflowing with antique purchases. His attitude towards OPM (Other People's Money) taught me not to cheat people or to be cheated. He never paid me back. Ever since, every interaction I've had with him has been on his side. In other words, I didn't benefit from it. From that point on, my trust would have to be earned.

I also must say that I was happy for my sisters to have those dresses. But that was a crummy thing for my Father to do. I've said throughout my life that I've been broke many times but never poor. That's in large part due to a promise I made to myself as a result of my Father's actions, that I would never be without money.

When I came to produce and distribute movies, I always said (and given this advice to others when asked) that I would never do a project I didn't believe in enough to mortgage my house, as I would come to do for THE BLOB.

Pennsylvania, a Quaker state, allowed no Sunday movies, sporting events, or large retail stores to be open on Sunday. Every Sunday, however, the Boyd Theatre at 19th and Chestnut Street in Philadelphia previewed the five top films to be released in the future weeks for the press and industry members. While the VIP screening started at 6:30 PM, the Harris family – Ben, Sara, my three sisters and me – were in attendance as the films were test-screened, starting at 7:00 AM. This helped the projectionists ready the varying sound systems then in use. We saw all of the biggest movies weeks ahead of release and couldn't wait for each Sunday to roll around.

The Depression arrived with devastating effect upon the economy and job market. Yet the movies prospered. People wanted to escape their troubles and could always find a quarter for a theatre ticket. Our family enjoyed a simple lifestyle. Aside from having one Christmas sans toys (which we received two weeks later), our sacrifices were bearable.

My Father continued night jobs for extra money showing movies to private parties at their homes or meeting rooms with his two portable, now 16mm, projectors. One night, when I was about fifteen he asked, "You know how to run a projector?"

I said, "Yes I do."

He said, "I find myself double booked tonight. I want you to run one of the shows."

I was thrilled.

He said, "Somebody will be here at 7:30 PM to pick you up and the film will be on the job. You just take the projector."

At 7:30 PM my Mother kissed me good-bye at the door, and wished me luck on my first private party job.

I was picked up by a police officer in uniform and I asked, "Where are you going?"

He said, "Oh, you didn't know. I'm going to the police headquarters meeting hall."

I thought, "Wow, my first private show job and it's with the Philadelphia Police Department."

I arrived and was almost blinded by the amount of brass there. I was introduced to the Chief of Police and several of his assistants. I was told that any time I was ready, the show could begin.

I went to the table, mounted the projector, threaded it up, called for lights out and started the show. I wondered what the show would be. Watching the screen, I saw a woman totally disrobed and sidled up to a man whose pants were coming off. It was an explicit, illegal, *pornographic* movie! I sat there concerned that this might have been a setup to take me into custody. Pornography was prohibited by all legal standards of the time. This was 1934, and we even had a State Board of Censors in Pennsylvania.

The police roared with enjoyment. When I wrapped up the film and projector, I was waiting to be busted. Instead, the chief handed me a fat envelope for delivery to my Father. The squad car escorted me home.

My Father showed up at the house about half an hour later as I was having a cup of tea with my Mother. He asked for his envelope, took out a $5 bill and handed it to me saying, "Not bad for one hours work." But he kept the other $95.00. This was in the period when family men were lucky to get $15 a week for forty-five hours of work. He asked how everything went. I told him about my worry concerning the film's content.

My Mother caught on immediately, and that's how my private show career terminated. Due to my disappointment with the financial arrangement, I was becoming more interested in legitimate show business.

The movie business awarded passes to its workers. Thanks to my Father's passes, most of my leisure time was spent in theatres, now functioning on Sundays due to the repeal of the blue laws preventing Sunday movies in this former Quaker state. I was enthralled by the movies and collected press books on most of the outstanding films. Press books were manuals issued by the studios to theatres and publicists to help promote each individual film. They contained biographies of stars and the director, proofs of each and every movie advertisement, and scripts for radio commercials. If my press book collection hadn't been destroyed in a fire years later in my parent's home, it would be worth a fortune today. I used my press book collection to illustrate a talk I gave as a Central High School student. It astonished my classmates. I became the gossip columnist on the high school newspaper, *The Centralizer.* It was a big thrill to watch people turn to my column when students picked up their weekly copies. I also had become quite an artist, adept at space layouts, lettering, and illustration. These talents became immeasurably helpful later in my movie theatre career.

While in Central High, I was a contributor to *The Philadelphia Record,* our morning newspaper. I occasionally drew caricatures of the various stars appearing in person at local theatres. I started taking my original drawings to the theatres where the stars were appearing and asking them to autograph them. At the Earle Theatre, young Gracie Allen graciously invited me into her dressing room and called George Burns from his dressing room to come and meet this "cute, young artist." We talked awhile and George said, "Okay kid, we have to go on soon."

I said, "Thank you very much for your time. I'll always be a fan."

Later, I met Mary Pickford as she was entering the Stage Door. She invited me over to a sitting area to talk. She was very pleased with my sketch of her and autographed it rather erratically. She smelled so much of alcohol that I didn't understand how she could form her words or walk straight.

Eddie Cantor was especially gracious. He thought he was better looking than my sketch, and I agreed with him. I have a picture somewhere of Eddie and I looking goo-goo eyed at each other.

One August day in 1934, I was waiting for the traffic light to change at the intersection of 16th and Market Streets in Philadelphia. I noticed that the light facing my intended crossing of Market Street stayed stubbornly red. I waited impatiently, and then heard some music approaching from the west. I turned to see the source of the music. It was coming from a small band preceding a large Phaeton-style automobile with the convertible top down. As the automobile neared 16th Street, I walked into the street for a better view and saw Franklin D. Roosevelt sitting in the backseat, smiling and waving to passersby who stopped to wave and applaud. I stepped aside for a secret service man who was running next to the car. It had stopped.

FDR smiling called out to me, "Come here young man." He held his arm out and I walked over to shake his hand. "What's your name?" he asked.

"Jack Harris, sir," I replied.

"Have a good day, Jack," he said as the car resumed its forward motion. All I remember doing was standing there in an overwhelmed state of surprise.

⌘

Chapter 5: Exhibition

In 1936, I was seventeen and finishing my summer job as counselor in the city operated camp for under-privileged children. My Father got me an interview to become an entry-level usher at a theatre nearing construction completion in North Philadelphia. The Mayfair Theatre was a true dream palace. It was brand new, containing state of the art equipment, air conditioning, seats, and dazzling décor. I was interviewed and immediately selected. I worked six days a week with Fridays off and earned the magnificent sum of $10.00 per week. The other ushers were paid $1 per day, and within a week I became the chief usher. I had four assistants. In those days when patrons arrived after the show started, they were politely ushered to their seats by a uniformed attendant holding a flashlight discreetly for them to see where they were going. How things have changed. Today, if you want to find an attendant, you have to leave the theatre and go to the doorman at the theatre entrance, who then calls a guy in custodian's clothing to help you, but not to seat you.

It is interesting that patrons in my usher days stood up to allow the late comers to enter the rows to find their seats. Today, you are not only in the dark, but you are tripping over the feet of lazy moviegoers, unwilling to stand up and let you by.

I diligently applied myself and learned the rudiments of running a successful theatre from the inside. I went from head usher to assistant manager in six months. It was during this period that I honed my business sense and developed the business acumen that's served me so well throughout my life. This came from dealing with cash collections each day and having a daily subsidiary expense. You learn to take on and juggle a lot from a business standpoint; that was a wonderful education for me.

The manager, Herb Schulman, allowed me to do any publicity stunt I could dream up. He got the credit for it, but I got the experience. One day, eighteen months later, he took very ill, and wound up with then-terminal double pneumonia.

I ran the theatre in his absence, and the boss noticed that all the promotions and publicity continued. One night the manager had taken a serious turn, and his end was near. Our boss, Mel Fox, showed up at the theatre to go with me to visit Herb. We got to his house and his wife met us in tears to announce that Herb had just passed away. I took it very hard, since Herb was my mentor and dear friend. The funeral took place two days later and in the car leaving the cemetery, Mel said to me, "Jack, you're the new manager."

I didn't tell him I was barely nineteen, but determined to be the best manager in the circuit of theatres.

One of my innovations was the enhanced Saturday matinee, four-hours of kiddie entertainment which included additional cartoons, an extra Western movie, and stunts such as tossing 100 Philadelphia soft pretzels to 1,000 ravenous kids. We also put on little skits interacting with the audience. My actor friends were a great help in this endeavor, also getting extra experience for themselves. The kids dubbed me Uncle Jack. That's how *Uncle Jack's Kiddie Show* was born. It was the best ten cent baby sitter available. Each Saturday matinee the house was always packed with kids in the aisles, on the floor, and when skinny enough, squeezing two in a seat.

One of my annual stunts was the Mayfair 4th of July Parade, which I originated with the help of the local civic and business leaders. It consisted of drum and bugle corps bands from the high school, Boy Scout troops, and church groups. I assembled horse drawn floats and rolling stock, plus assorted kids and adults dressed in historic uniforms. The spirit was wonderful. Everybody turned out to participate in or witness the parade.

I was on a pickup truck with a cameraman supplied by my Father's friend, Lou Kellman, who owned News Reel Laboratories. They were in the business of supplying film records of all the local news and sporting events at the time that were edited into weekly newsreels. We filmed the parade and then were able to exhibit the results for two days following the event. It didn't matter what movies we were playing. Hundreds of people who had taken part in or had been watching the parade from the sidewalks came to see themselves on the big screen. I narrated the film and was able to dub in the music, all on a 78 RPM disc, which were popular at the time. It was a real satisfaction to join the crowds in the theatre and hear myself narrate the parade.

One day in 1938, my Father came home crest-fallen. The company where he had worked for twenty-five years ran out of movie suppliers and film franchisers and thus closed its doors. He was without employment, except for his now very occasional private showings. We talked over what would come next for him, and I suggested he reopen and take over the management of the company. He moaned, "That would cost at least $2,000.00."

I told him to contact his flamboyant friend, Lou Kellman, and see if he would want to be a partner. Lou agreed to back my Father in the enterprise and also put $1,000 on the table. My Father turned to me and said, "Where am I going to get the other $1,000.00?"

I had carefully put away $1,200 in my savings account and got him a $1,000 draft so he could make good on his share. I figured it was my Father. When he realized who had put half the money in, my Father asked me where I had gotten the $1,000.

I said, "Well, I didn't steal it. I saved it."

He said, "I really appreciate it. I want you to know that. I really do appreciate it."

My Father reopened the office and with the vaults full of old features, serials and short subjects, he started leasing films for Saturday matinees at $10.00 each. He was able to get together the basis of an ongoing distribution setup. When the exhibitors saw Benny, they knew he had old films. They also knew that they could get a bargain.

I helped him by polishing up some of the old dust-laden titles and inducing my theatre manager friends to get in there and take advantage of Benny Harris, to his delight. My Father couldn't stand to have any partners, so it only took him two years to get rid of his partner, Lou Kellman, but four years to pay me back.

I never made a profit from any of the business dealings I went into with my Father. Sometimes I got paid back. But as I was getting more successful, and he wasn't, every dealing I had with him was like this: I got a "thank you very much," and that was it! That was my relationship with him. Maybe it was jealously. I don't know what it was. He used to find and share so much joy with my sisters. When it came to me, it was all harsh criticism and judgment.

One warm spring day in 1939, I was leaving the printer that did my weekly programs for the Mayfair Theatre, and walking up Vine Street toward my Father's office at American Film Company. I noticed an unusually well dressed couple walking toward me. He was a tall, dapper, older man with a healthy gait. She was an elegant lady about a head shorter than her escort. As I approached them, something about them looked very familiar. But after all, I was on Vine Street in Philadelphia, PA, and although this was film row at that time, I didn't anticipate bumping into any stellar luminaries.

The man nodded to me and his lady smiled at me, so I said what you'd say under those circumstances – "Hello."

The gentleman said, "Perhaps you can help us?"

They didn't look at all shabby enough to be asking for a hand out. So, I said, "What can I do for you?"

He said, "We're looking for a small screening room."

I noticed a parcel under his arm. I said, "Well, you ought to be happy that you asked me because I know a screening room a few steps away from here. Come on. I'll take you to it."

I opened the door and let them into the waiting room of my Fathers's office. He had a habit of standing next to his desk and talking on the telephone. That enabled him to see what was going on outside through the big picture window looking onto the street.

He quickly ended his conversation and looked up at me and said, "Hi ya' stranger. What brings you to these parts?"

I said, "I just left the print shop and was headed for my car when I bumped into a couple of friends of mine."

I said to the gentleman, "I want you to meet my Father, Ben Harris, who is the proprietor, and also a gifted projectionist with a private screening room at the top of those stairs."

My Father came forward a little puzzled and said, "How do you do? My name is Ben Harris. My son wasn't courteous enough to give me your names. What are they?"

The gentleman shyly said, "I'm David Griffith."

They shook hands. He then introduced his wife. That rang a bell.

I said, "Mr. Griffith."

He said, "Call me David, Jack."

I asked, "Is your middle initial by any chance, W?"

He smiled broadly and answered, "Yes, I'm D.W. Griffith."

And I said, "BIRTH OF A NATION."

I noticed my Father almost startled off his feet to be in the presence of the icon who produced not only BIRTH OF A NATION, but also many other memorable films.

I said, "I have to leave, but I'm sure my Father can take care of you."

We said our good-byes and I went to my car happy to be a movie man headed out to my theatre.

In the '30s, the screen show consisted of a newsreel, a cartoon, and if enough time, a ten-to-twenty minute short subject, or mini-movie, about topics ranging from hygiene to sports to aviation to human interest. In 1939, at the age of twenty, I entered an exploitation contest for the best publicity and advertising campaign for a movie in any motion picture theatre. I put on a magnificent campaign for MAISIE, a movie starring Ann Sothern, supported by a Pete Smith short subject. Smith was the reigning comedy narrator of the day. I spent many hours of planning.

Stunts I conceived of included a MAISIE poster embedded in a block of ice parked on the spacious sidewalk in front of the theater. Contestants would win free tickets if they could guess when the ice would melt and the poster could be safely retrieved. I also selected the highest traffic store in the shopping street to place a continuous projector in its window showing scenes from the movie. The local restaurant featured a MAISIE menu, which contained a plug for the movie. Finally, on the last night of the show, I advertised that a real live baby would be given away free to the holder of the lucky ticket stub. I was on stage announcing the winning number, and I heard a scream from the audience. We had "planted" the winning ticket with Mrs. Murphy, the neighborhood busybody, coming up to claim the baby. I made her promise to keep the baby in good health and give it a lot of love and attention. Before a packed house, she nervously agreed. Then I called an usher from the wings who had the bundle of squirming joy wrapped in a blanket, which I presented to Mrs. Murphy after lifting the blanket and exposing the cutest face of a real, live baby pig.

I won the exploitation contest first prize for feature promotion and also first prize for promotion of the Pete Smith short subject. They were both from MGM Studios, then the epitome of Hollywood dream factories. I converted the prize into a roundtrip train ride to Hollywood and used what was left for expenses.

My Pennsylvania Railroad lower berth was a revelation. It was my first sleeper train trip, lasting four days. I had to go to New York to catch the 20th Century Limited which took me to Chicago and then on to San Francisco with stop offs in between. When I arrived in Los Angeles, it was one of my lifetime thrills to be walking through the then new Spanish décor Union Station. I was met by the one-and-only Pete Smith, who became my guide for the trip.

My first day at MGM began with a trip on the open-air studio shuttle, where I shared a ride with young Lana Turner to Stage 23 and the LITTLE NELLIE KELLY set. I watched a scene being shot, and at the

Jack (Right) with Judy Garland and Douglas McPhail on Little Nellie Kelly set, 1939.

wrap was taken out to the front lawn and photographed with my idol, Judy Garland and her co-star, Douglas McPhail. The studio still photographer posed us as an arm-in-arm trio walking toward camera.

Judy said to me, "We're Spencer Tracy, Jeanette Macdonald and Clark Gable."

We all cracked up at the meaning of her one-liner, which aped the photograph currently in newspapers everywhere of the famous stars of the movie SAN FRANCISCO.

I met all of the stars working in the various films being shot at the time, including Lionel Barrymore and Lou Ayres making the Young Dr. Kildare movie. Groucho Marx almost ran me over as he was being chauffeured to his set. I saw Mickey Rooney on the way to a rehearsal, and Helen Hayes in the commissary.

I also visited Paramount Studio and RKO Studio. Sadly, Fred Astaire, my favorite, was not working in anything that day. I met Anna Nagel and Richard Carlson who were shooting SWEET LITTLE ALICE BLUE GOWN. I spent each evening going to sneak previews in nearby cities where I learned about observing audience reaction. Several of the films I had seen being made had been taken back for reshooting and editing. When I later viewed them, they had been greatly improved.

As I was being driven to the Union Station for my return home, Pete Smith asked me if there was anything else he could do. I replied, "Yes, I want to stay and work in Hollywood, can you help me?"

Pete said, "Go back to Philadelphia, kid. Work your ass off and let Hollywood send for you. When they do, you'll come back here in glory, and they'll pay any price you ask."

I returned to Philadelphia and found my boss, Melvin Fox, very jealous of my Hollywood sojourn. After spending four years under his super-tyrannical rule, I figured it was time to take what I knew and had accomplished and set up shop elsewhere. I found an open door at Milgram Theatres. David Milgram, the President of the company, treated me with such respect, admiration, and financial reward that I would do anything he asked of me. I had a big hand in booking the various films we showed at my Avenue Theatre in Germantown, where I was also given free hand with publicity and advertising. The Dave Milgram/Jack H. Harris combination was dynamite. The time I spent with Milgram Theatres was the best exhibition experience of my life.

My Father had acquired a new low budget film called I'LL SELL MY LIFE. I booked it into my theatre and did a MAISIE-style campaign. One of the main gags was the continuous projector placed in the window of the major store in the area, which was only one block away. The box office results were good for my theatre and also gave my Father a model with which to distribute the picture successfully in the entire territory. I quickly became publicity director for twenty theatres, distinguishing myself with many publicity stunts to include a 1941 fund drive for a major charity, chaired by Dave Milgram. It featured a black-tie dinner appearance by honored guest, Eleanor Roosevelt, who I so looked forward to meeting. I loved working in and around movies. My life in doing so, was only moving onward and upward.

On a weekend trip to Baltimore, to visit my cousins, I met Muriel Goodman, a nice pretty Jewish girl, through my cousin, Florence Shockett. We had great times together and saw a lot of each other when I would visit Baltimore on occasion. I was attracted to Muriel and her witty charm and grace. My feelings were influenced by the elegant home and loving aura of her parents' attentions. Her family lived the style I admired and to which I aspired. I was hoping I could attain this lifestyle through my promising career in the movies.

⌘

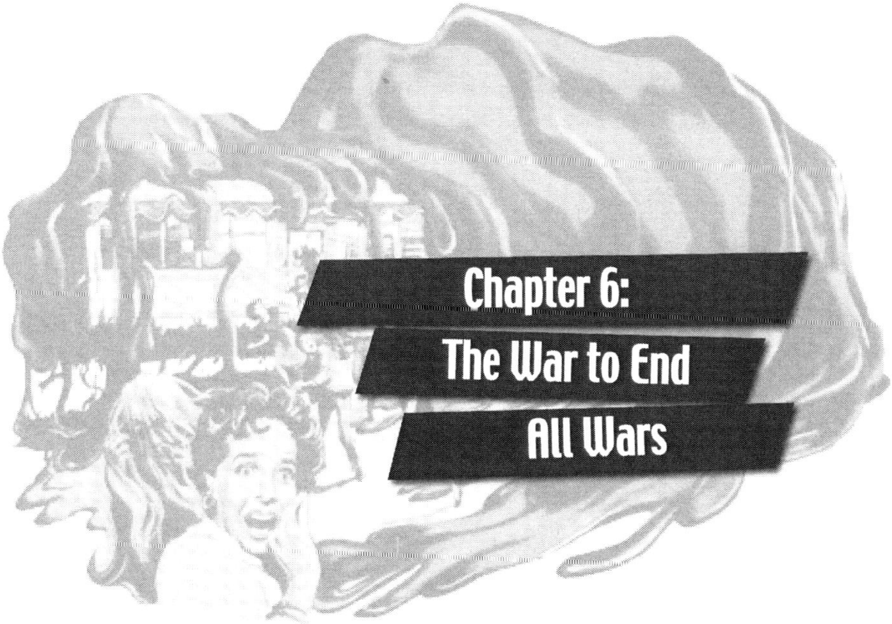

Chapter 6: The War to End All Wars

My future plans were slightly altered by a massive upheaval. Hitler had advanced upon Poland, Czechoslovakia, and Austria while menacing Western Europe with bombing raids. An offer was made to those of us who were of draft age by the U.S. Government to avoid the draft by enlisting for one year in the Armed Services. I joined many thousands in taking advantage of this offer by enlisting in the U.S. Army in June, 1941. The USA was not at war. I was to report for enlistment in September. I celebrated my potential army enlistment by quitting my job and heading to New York via train to catch a boat for a two-week cruise to Miami and Havana.

The S.S. Mexico, a very well-appointed ship, stopped first in Miami Beach, where we cruisers spent two days sunning among the palm trees getting to know each other. I had teamed up with a comely New Jersey gal named Terry, and other couples who had formed. Then off for a two-day stay in Havana. The "manager" (me) was drafted to program our itinerary. I hired a chauffeured Hispano Souisa limousine to take us on a custom sightseeing tour. After hours of museums, churches, and famous edifices, the chauffer said to me, "Señor, when are you going to see the famous Cuban Circus?"

I incredulously admitted that I had never heard of the circus.

"That is número uno to the usual touristas," he said. He explained that the show was sexy and very adult.

My car-mates quickly demanded to be taken to the circus forthwith. We were ushered into a plush "club." After a rum and Coca-Cola, we were let into a smaller, mirrored salon holding six chairs facing a 10x12 foot platform.

As soon as we were seated, the rhumba music began and three gorgeous, scantily clad couples danced in through a mirrored door. They exuberantly performed their Latin dance without missing a beat, and as the dance ended, they were all nude. We applauded frantically.

A well-dressed announcer appeared and explained that a special starring routine was about to be performed by a lad and lady of our choosing. The sextet looked fantastic, yet we patrons soon selected the couple of our choice. The eliminated four exited, and the chosen couple elegantly performed every act of intercourse imaginable. I was fascinated, and then my attention strayed to the reflections of our group in the mirror. Terry looked away from the performance. She caught the act from the corner of her eye. My accompanying friend, Jim, looked at the floor in embarrassment. The others joined me in marveling at the performance. In half-an-hour the show ended with a quiet group of six patrons sitting there. Then the announcer offered a private encounter with either of our stars, or with one of the eliminated dancers. We all embarrassedly declined. The balance of our Havana stay was memorable.

Muriel and I resumed our relationship on my return to Philadelphia. We spent numerous romantic dates together in Baltimore and really got to know each other. I duly reported for army duty in September 1941, and was shipped to Camp Croft, South Carolina. On a weekend pass, which I overstayed, I joined Muriel for a thrilling get-together, during which we decided to get married.

I returned to camp and was taken into custody for being two days late. I was in solitary where it dawned upon me that my movements were no longer at my exclusive option. I became as close to depressed as ever in my life. The next day my company commander remanded me to his office to explain my absence. I told him the truth about my elopement and promised never again to violate the army rules. He expressed sympathy in view of my outstanding record and decreed, "one day in solitary," to compensate for my being AWOL. I never forgot it.

My last week of basic training at Camp Croft, fell on December 7th, 1941. Right after Reveille, we heard the radio announcements of the Japanese sneak attack on Pearl Harbor. We knew this automatically extended our one-year enlistment indefinitely. We were sent to a Fort Dix, New Jersey staging area to await orders to join the first European Convoy of WWII. I was much closer to Baltimore and saw Muriel whenever possible.

We were assigned to the S.S. Mexico, the very same boat on which I'd cruised to Havana just one year before. We were 105 passengers then, and now our converted troop ship held 2,000 of us, four bunks high. I knew the ship thoroughly. When fresh water baths were prohibited for water conservation, another GI, Joe Gohegan, and I alternately stood watch at a private bathroom in one of the hallways where we each enjoyed a hot, fresh water shower daily.

We both volunteered for the Mess Hall, which operated from 5:00 AM to 1:00 AM in order to feed all of the required three squares a day. The lines of hungry GIs were constant during the hours of operation. Joe and I were able to eat our meals at regular hours because we worked in the Mess Hall.

We were in the 34th Division and I wound up as a radio operator in the field artillery unit. Our convoy consisted of fourteen ships including two destroyers and a damage control ship. Things were going along fairly well in spite of crowded conditions.

Our convoy was on a zigzag route between the U.S. and Northern Ireland. A trip that normally would have taken five-and-a-half days was now scheduled for fourteen days. On the ninth day we were bedded down in our bunks when there was a thunderous explosion that rocked the ship. It was quickly determined that a German Sub had torpedoed us.

We had drilled every day for such an eventuality and began climbing into our overcoats and overshoes to stay as warm as possible in the icy Atlantic in our life rafts. Awaiting assembly orders we stood at the ready in the hold when there was another unnerving slam that again shook the ship. Suddenly the whole trap door opened to the night sky. By this time all of the lights in the hold were on breaching security because our company commander panicked as he came out the open trap door. He was in nervous shock as we helped him down the ladder and quickly closed the trapdoor. He kept explaining that all he was worried about were his men, and the worry was reciprocal.

Panic was spreading through our hold area. At that moment, I experienced the realization that losing my head was of no purpose. Thus, I remained perfectly calm. It was as though I had always known that I would survive any hazardous experience that might come my way. I felt a sense of destiny. Not for one second was I afraid of dire consequences, and I immediately set about spreading that calm.

The lights went out and we got our assembly instructions over the PA system. As we were heading out of the hold onto the deck there were at least four explosions that seemed distant from us. We later learned our destroyers had done their job and had sunk the German sub.

We were boarded by damage control crews and were sent back to our bunks while the repairs were being made. This was our only mishap, although we were alert to repeat attack possibility.

The night before we landed, the Captain ordered me to meet him in his stateroom. He asked me to sit down and excitedly started making an official sounding speech, which he interrupted himself by saying, "Harris, bullshit with the formalities. You're one hell of a soldier, and I thank you for your attitude and help. You're one of my best boys."

I sat in my bunk later and wrote the captain a "thank you" note, reciting some of my civilian career highlights and asking him to look out for an army opportunity to take advantage of my experiences.

We landed safely in Northern Ireland where cheering, grateful citizens of the realm greeted us. I still remember the thrilling feeling of marching in formation carrying our full regalia of helmets, backpacks, and rifles. I remember the sound of assembled crowds of Irish men and women shouting, "Hurray for the Yanks. Now we're going to win this war and stop the blitz." We couldn't yell back because we were in parade formation. Still, it was an incredible thing, to be surrounded by spontaneous cheering.

Now the real work began as we started our combat training. Two weeks of my basic training before the voyage included an advanced course at radio school, where I was certified as a radio operator using Morse code. We were a field artillery battalion and my potential combat job was to be in charge of the heavy guns. I was to observe their hits and radio back to the Gunnery crew of any needed shifts in their aim. The weeks went by, but I never saw any radio equipment.

We were encamped from place to place training for action and setting up our two-to-a-tent bedrolls on the bare, cold ground. As we began touring the area on the lookout for potential enemies, we were quickly becoming hardened to the difficulties of combat life.

Our division had been selected to conduct the frontal assault on Oran, North Africa, then in the hands of the Nazis. About three weeks into our commando training, about 100 of us were double timing up a hill loaded down with full equipment including gas masks, when one of my buddies nearby said, "Harris, I think they're calling you."

I questioned, "Who's calling me?"

He said, "Someone in that jeep down there."

I turned around and saw two MP's sitting in a jeep, indeed, yelling my name. I slowly descended to the jeep and said, "What is it?"

The MP Sergeant said, "You Private Harris?"

I replied, "Yes."

"What's your serial number and let me see your dog tags?"

When I satisfied his request, he told me to get into the back seat. I wondered why.

He said, "It's an order."

I turned around and saw my puzzled buddies who had halted going up the hill watching this encounter. I waved goodbye as I was being driven off.

We stopped at a company headquarters where there was much activity. I was asked to unload my weapon, put away my gas mask, and go into a waiting van. I said, "I think I'm allowed to know where I'm going and what this is all about."

The van driver said, "You've been ordered to a secret location. That's all I know."

I said, "Why can't I sit up here with you?"

He said, "You're not supposed to see where you are going."

I stepped into the windowless van and saw the doors being locked behind me. It was completely dark in there. I had my flashlight, until they quickly made me put it out. I was sitting in the dark, bumping over Northern Ireland country roads for the better part of an hour.

The van stopped. The doors opened. I was helped out with all my equipment, which had been scattered throughout the back of the van, my eyes still readjusting to the light. I saw a pristine marching field in front of a glorious castle. We were in Ballymena at the former summer retreat of the Queen of England (Queen Mum), now home to 300 British female army recruits. There were only a few of the uniformed women in sight when I arrived. I was immediately escorted to a series of billets where we would sleep and rest. There was also a Mess Hall complete with potato peeling and dish washing machines. My first joyous thought was, "As long as I'm here, I won't have to peel any more potatoes." I had experienced more than enough KP duty up to this time.

I entered my Billet and found a few GI's reading or doing chores. I asked one of them, "What the hell is this place?"

He rattled off, "It's the U.S. reppel deppel." The others started laughing.

I noticed there were real bunks. The floor was carpeted. There were sheets and blankets on the beds and pillows. I thought "Whatever I'm here for, I'll finally have some comfort."

As I put my things down on the bunk assigned to me, the door opened and the First Sergeant with a clipboard in hand asked, "Private Harris?"

I replied, "Yes sir."

"Follow me."

He took me to the reception office where the Camp Commandant, Colonel Harris, (no relation) greeted me.

The colonel said, "Let's assume that Private Harris doesn't know why he's here. You fill him in."

The First Sergeant, very amicably and not at all in the gruff demeanor of a usual first sergeant, explained to me that I had been transferred to the U.S. Replacement Depot (repple depple) where we were to train U.S. nationals who had enlisted in the services of other friendly countries before the U.S. got into the war. They were now being allowed to transfer in grade into the U.S. Armed Forces, retaining whatever rank they had achieved before at triple their foreign armed forces salary – a deal authored by president Franklin Delano Roosevelt.

The empty billets would house the transferees for two weeks of indoctrination into the customs and regimen facing them in their newly assigned U.S. Army positions.

I had been recommended by my former company commander as an excellent instructor who had artistic ability. I was to conduct classes daily in a curriculum that the other instructors and I would put together for this special training purpose. They issued me an armband with two stripes on it informing me that I was an acting Corporal. I figured they did it because the new student officers might not have respect for a buck private ordering them around.

Within two weeks, the other ten instructors and I got together a training program with a menu of subjects and supporting lecture detail. One of my jobs was to put together visual aids illustrating the various ranks and their metal symbols – star for general, eagle for colonel, etc. I also volunteered for leading callisthenic sessions and close order drill. I had been an exercise nut since I was fourteen, when I learned from our

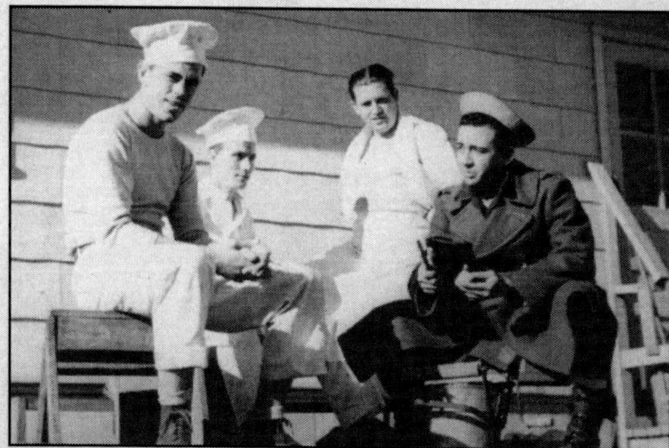

At Mess Hall. (Far right)

2nd Lieutenant, Jack H. Harris, graduates first in his class, 1943.

At WWII Sharpshooting Practice

Private Jack H. Harris

Private Jack Harris (Far right), the author and the director, gave the cast a pep talk just before the performance of "Hello, Hello."

gym instructor how to avoid aging and stay in shape in later years by doing at least thirty pushups daily. I still do them every day.

One day, we eleven instructors were given ten minutes to assemble in front of the castle. Colonel Harris called, "Ten-hut!" We all snapped to attention and witnessed King George, Queen Mum, and princesses, teenaged Elizabeth, and her younger sister Margaret Rose, all in uniform and shook hands with them. They were here to visit the British recruits and stopped to visit us yanks. Every time through the years when I see photos of Queen Elizabeth, I'm reminded of this fortuitous happening.

Months later, after graduating about 3,000 officers, I was on the parade ground with about fifty officer recruits, putting them through a very precise military close order drill. I was dressed in my usual fresh pressed uniform, including shiny boots and a proper uniform cap. A staff car pulled up in the distance with its occupants observing us. I went about my business putting the officers through their paces, when I noticed the staff car chauffer open the rear door to let out an officer of General rank.

I immediately called "Halt," to my men and shouted, "Attennshun!"

As the General approached the platform where I was standing, I couldn't believe my eyes. It was General Breshon B. Somerville, adjutant to Ike Eisenhower, Supreme Allied Commander of all the Forces in Europe. He was wearing a big smile. When he came up on the platform and stood before me, I sharply saluted him and he saluted me back.

He said, "Corporal, I'm here on an inspection tour. Would you mind if I said a few words?"

I replied, "I'm sure that everybody here would be thrilled to hear from you, sir."

He got on the mike and welcomed the assemblage to the U.S. Army and wished them Godspeed in their efforts to assist in the war effort. Then he said, "By the way, that's a soldier," – pointing to me. "What's your name?"

"Jack H. Harris, sir."

His aide took down my name and serial number and the General shook hands with me as he left to the cheers of the officer transferees on the field.

"We're here to welcome you and to wish you luck in rejoining our forces. If all the instructors are as capable as Corporal Harris, you'll have a proper time in the army."

I called attention. We all saluted. The General said to me, "Good work."

"Thank you, Sir." I replied.

The British, who were our hosts at Repple Depple, invited the American contingent to a number of entertainments, and we reciprocated by putting on a U.S. Show which I produced, directed and performed in, with the help of British corporal Al Berlin, nephew of our famous Irving. My vaudeville experience came in handy. The show was strictly for the Armed Forces then stationed at Ballymena Castle. Our show was to thank the Brits for their splendid hospitality.

When the show was over, Commandant Colonel Harris congratulated me on a good performance and said that I had just been approved by General Eisenhower to go back to New Jersey. I was to go to Officer Candidate School where I should acquire my Officer rank. He handed me the orders from the Supreme Allied Command. Evidently, the General had enjoyed my performance on the exercise field.

I arrived in the USA via the good ship Queen Elizabeth, in mid-December, 1942. This was a great surprise to my family, as security did not allow any announcement of my homecoming. This proved to be a very fortuitous piece of timing. My wife Muriel was now in her eighth month of pregnancy. With good luck I could be back home in time to witness the birth of my first child.

Muriel had grown quite a bit around the middle, now a mere fourteen days away from delivery. We welcomed our daughter Lynda into the world on January 2, 1943 in Baltimore, Maryland. Becoming a father was wonderful for me. I always knew it meant that I had a chance to be a good father. I just had to do the opposite of what my Father did.

Muriel, Lynda, and I were ensconced in our first home, a brand new, first floor, one bedroom apartment in Arlington, Virginia, twenty minutes from my office at the Army Security Agency. We were surrounded by Army, Navy and Air Force brass families, all pledged to help get the conflagration over with so we could resume our places in civilian life.

I picked up my Mother one morning, who had come by train from Philadelphia. She was suitably overwhelmed on seeing the Pentagon on the way to our abode, yet more excited to see our apartment and her year-old granddaughter, Lynda.

We spent a wonderful day together. On the way back to the train station she handed me a ring box as a token of her pride on the way I handled my army career. I opened the box in the station to discover an antique Italian, solid gold lion head ring with a one-carat diamond in his mouth. I appreciated antiquities and marveled at the size and clarity of the diamond.

"That's from my engagement ring," my Mother said. I promised to cherish and value it for the rest of my life. The lion ring never leaves my right pinky, and has helped identify me through my many adventures.

In late 1943, I was called to a meeting with a Colonel in charge of Internal Security for the OSS. He asked me to do a check on the office preparing the grand plan for D-Day. My job as a spy was to purchase from the Army/Navy store an insignia as Lieutenant Colonel. I was then to doctor up my security badge to be renamed John Haversham, expert in preservation and protection of electronic equipment. The following order was to execute a specific order to steal the plans for the landing and dispersal of equipment and supplies for the Normandy invasion. I was to be assisted by Lt. Jerry Canellan, a fellow ASA member, with additional orders to work out our own plan for this job.

He was also cleared for top-secret information. He was to be the outside man ("Colonel Canfield"), and I would be the inside man. Jerry "cased" the top-secret location inside the Pentagon, where the commanding general was holding forth to make sure that when I showed up, no one would have ever seen me before, allowing me to successfully play my role. With our research completed, "Colonel Canfield" phoned the commanding general and told him that Lt. Colonel Haversham, an electronics preservation expert, would be in to advise him on that aspect of the battle plans.

I duly arrived and had to go through two armed guards in the entry office, and then into an anteroom manned by a major, then into the Sanctum Sanctorum where the General had his office. I was greeted with courtesy and I asked about ten vital questions about the operation, all of which were top secret.

In the middle of the tenth question, the Major came running in and said, "General, sir, you're wanted at once in an emergency meeting at general staff headquarters."

The General excused himself and told me to look around. He took the Major with him. I knew the meeting wouldn't last long and my time was severely limited. There I was in the candy store of miniature boats, jeeps, Landing Ship Vehicles, armaments and other paraphernalia for the invasion, all laid out in a tabletop reproduction of the Normandy coast. To the left of it were two big, thick telephone book sized manuals stamped TOP SECRET D-Day plans.

I took one and put it under my jacket, walking as calmly as I could through the anteroom. I received a nice salute from the two armed guards standing at the entrance. I shifted into high gear for my rendezvous with Lt. Canellan and the OSS Colonel who clapped me on the shoulder with congratulations and took the target book into his briefcase.

Lt. Canellan and I were ushered out of a secret entrance to a waiting staff car and sped away to the Army Security Agency in Arlington, Virginia. I was thrilled to be promoted to the rank of First Lieutenant.

A week later Lt. Canellan and myself were silent invitees to a lecture by the OSS Colonel to a big selection of army brass. Our accomplishment was minutely detailed to the audience, but our identities remained as secret as the operation. The careless Pentagon General was retired to a post in Kansas City with the understanding that he would be allowed to resign upon the cessation of hostilities.

The Army Security Agency and OSS chores were very stressful and after completing two-and-a-half years of it, I asked for reassignment. Once again, I was told, "Here's what's available. You pick your job."

I selected Holabird Signal Depot in Baltimore, MD, because that's where my family was at the time. In 1944 they made me Public Information Officer for the Third Service Command.

Victory in Europe Day occurred on May 8th, 1945. I had accumulated double the required points for separation from the service should the war end. My last chore was taking General "Skinny" Wainright to a bond drive in Philadelphia. Skinny was the Three Star General Assistant to General Douglas MacArthur. He had been left to defend Bataan when MacArthur took off in the night for Australia to establish his new headquarters in Sydney. General Wainright lost his hearing due to the intense pounding of Japanese artillery as they were softening up the American forces for their triumphal takeover by the Japanese Imperial Army. Skinny spent three years as a POW before being freed.

Our tour included a parade down Broad Street where my twin sisters just happened to be standing in front of Temple University where they were coeds. Mitzie and Dotzie couldn't believe their eyes as our car went by and they discovered their brother in the seat in front of General Wainright. They didn't even know I was in Philadelphia, let alone appearing in a parade on Broad Street in such good company.

Our tour concluded with a pit stop at a beautiful restroom building in Fairmount Park. I went into the urinal room, where I noticed that the Governor of Pennsylvania and the Mayor of Philadelphia were on my left, and General Wainright and his navy rear admiral son were on my right, lined up at the urinals. The Governor leaned over to me and said, "One thing my grandmother taught me is if you're in public life, take advantage of every opportunity to piss in private."

A few weeks after Victory Day, when the exit scores were being tallied for rotation in separating us from the service, my score was among the highest. I was on a bond drive in Richmond, Virginia where a huge golf tournament was in progress, when I received a Teletype giving me my separation date.

On October 24, 1945, my family was increased by the arrival of, my son, Anthony. I had a lot to be thankful for. I had completed four-and-a-half years in the service, and was now eager to get back to my profession and my family. In the weeks I had to formally leave my uniform, I puzzled over what my next career move would be. I was separated from the service on November 10, 1945, and proceeded to Philadelphia to rent a house and await my wife Muriel, daughter Lynda, and son Anthony to come from Baltimore and join me for Thanksgiving (and my birthday) celebration.

In summing up this chapter of my life, I was recently asked what lessons I took from the Army that most benefited my career in movies. As I mentioned before, working my way up the ranks in theaters helped me hone my business sense. My time in the Army helped me hone my attention to detail. From the ground up, there isn't a detail of a production, job, or deal that I don't pour over and look at fastidiously. There's only one kind of deal, and that's a deal that's fair on both sides. But you need to know the deal from the ground up. I think, if pressed, that I could also do any job on a film set if need be. Because I knew that to produce movies successfully, I had to learn my way around a production from the ground up. In my time in the Army, I never would have heard, "By the way – That's a soldier" if I hadn't been committed to every little detail of my uniform, stature, march, and everything else that went into it from the ground up. I took that skill set and put it into my career in the film industry.

⌘

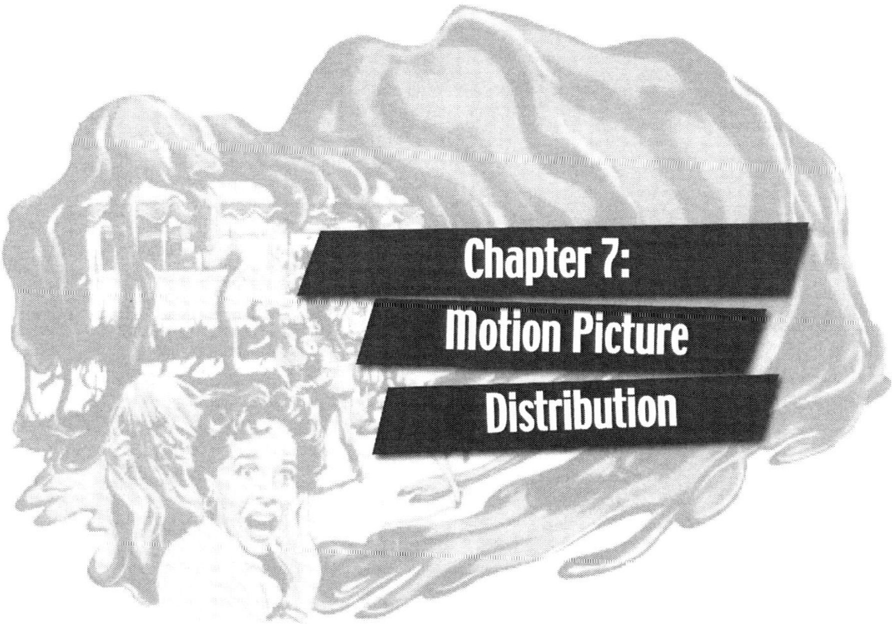

Chapter 7: Motion Picture Distribution

Counterintuitively or not, it was the Great Depression that spawned the Golden Age of Hollywood. It was the best relief to forget your troubles, in the darkened theatre, entertained by the lavish lifestyles shown in the popular movies of the day. Stars were born and matured in the Studio System. When I eventually became a theatre manager, I was always surprised by a patron walking in and handing his twenty-five cent ticket to the doorman and saying to me, "What's playing tonight?" Fortunately, movies had become a habit, making people wealthy in all aspects of the motion picture industry. The studios prospered, and as they did they built more and more theatres, which back then they still owned.

Production, distribution, and exhibition were the first real monopoly in this industry. This meant that a new exhibitor with a brand new, gorgeous theatre had to wait to get a new movie until all the theatres that pre-existed it were finished with the film. These new exhibitors banded together and sued the major studios for not allowing them to bid for an earlier run of their films. The government soon stepped in with a divorcement decree that the studios would either have production and distribution, or production and exhibition, but not all three. This led to a massive divestiture of theatres by the various studios, creating a whole new method of distribution, whereby any theatre with the financial ability to do so could outbid its rivals for the first showing of a new film. This rule has been relaxed in the past twenty years or so, and now studios again have minor interests in theatre chains throughout the country; however, there is no longer a monopoly.

While theatres have been the primary source of revenue for new films, the evolution of new distribution media has given us television, which became a venue for films that had played in theatres, three years or older. This three year rule became steadily eroded until twelve-to-fifteen months became the norm. All of this had reduced the movie theatre going public substantially through the years, since there was now another way to see and enjoy filmed entertainment in your own home. My children and I viewed television with great delight, while I became concerned for the future of theatrical exhibition. In this regard, I echoed the fears of the major studios.

Pondering how I was going to support my family, I came to an absolute decision that I wouldn't be working in the theatres anymore. It was a seven-day-a-week ordeal, with the most important workdays being Saturdays, Sundays, and holidays, I was no longer going to be working when everybody else was out having fun. I planned to devote weekends to my family. Offers came in for theatre jobs, which I rejected. Then I considered offers to do publicity at various offices with connections to Hollywood studios. Talking things over with my Father, he asked me, "Why work for anybody else when you can work with me, and we could build a good, solid business together?"

My first thought was, "Do I go for this bullshit again?"

I agreed to work with him for 25% of the profits. He had the investment of all the equipment necessary, plus the office building location which was in the heart of Film Row.

I spent my time improving and solidifying my Fathers's small, independent distributing office by acquiring new releases and dusting off old ones with new titles and campaigns. We were doing about

$1,200.00 a week in rentals, but we didn't keep that much money. As laid out in our deals, we were giving 60% of that back to the producer. The movie was always a producer's investment upon which he needed a return. I continued working hard, getting us up to doing about $5,000.00 a week of business.

While I was sitting in the office one day, a very dapper, little gentleman came in and asked for Benny Harris. His name was Mr. Kendis. He and my Father walked into the back office for half an hour. Then my Father suddenly appeared and took me out front on the sidewalk for privacy as he asked, "Can we resurrect the 1932 movie, THE NEW ADVENTURES OF TARZAN?" This was a very primitive movie made by Edgar Rice Burrows and starring former Olympics champion Herman Brix as Tarzan. Brix later adopted the stage name Bruce Bennett, and appeared in a dozen movies and TV series.

I answered, "Yes, get it!"

My Father said, "But I have to pay him $150.00."

I knew that our old reissues were bringing in $12.50 to $25 a booking and calculated that we could certainly get twenty bookings even for Saturday matinee shows. I still said, "Get it."

When Mr. Kendis came out with my Father to the front office, my Father introduced him to me and he was very gracious. He congratulated me on sticking with the family before leaving.

I asked my Father whether we now owned the distribution rights to the picture for our territory outright. He answered, "Yes, for one year."

I asked another questions, "Why don't you give him $300.00 and own it in perpetuity?"

He replied, "Are you crazy? Mr. Kendis owns the negative."

I was incredulous. "We can make more money if you don't have to see Mr. Kendis every year for permission." That was the day I learned that the only thing positive in this business is the *negative.*

Right after that, I tricked up a splendid campaign for the TARZAN movie. We earned our investment money back from the first matinee that appeared in a small theatre on Market Street in Philadelphia. It played five weeks and we earned $5,000.00 net for the $150.00 investment. Even my dad who had seen "everything" was astonished. We distributed the picture for a number of years. There were many small time reissues and several big time ones that made the business grow from $500.00 a week to $5,000.00 a week on the average. Yet, my take home pay was only $150.00 a week.

One day, lightening struck, and we beat all others to the reissue rights to David O. Selznick's PRISONER OF ZENDA, GARDEN OF ALLAH, and TOM SAWYER. I really wanted TOM SAWYER, but had to take the other two to get it. With TOM SAWYER, I had been able to pack the house on a slow Monday night by running a contest for the best-costumed person representing the lead character from the movie. We had lots of Tom imitators and their families happily filling the seats.

Charles Casanave was Selznick's partner in the reissue business. To his credit, he never forgot what I did with TOM SAWYER as a reissue. The new campaign I put together consisted of J.C. Penny giving each theatre participating in the contest a new two-wheeler and a number of subsidiary prizes, which were all displayed for weeks in advance in one of their prominent street-facing windows. The newspaper was printing daily Human Interest stories about the kids and all the effort they were expending to win the prizes, even including photographs.

The theatres treated the movie like a brand new blockbuster and were rewarded at the box office, especially when the whole family bought tickets to see their contestant win.

In 1949, after almost four years of hard work, my family still lived in a little row house. Meanwhile my Father had graduated from a small apartment to an impressive townhouse, built in 1790 on Clinton Street in Philadelphia, which he and my Mother filled with precious 18th century antiques. He also drove her around in a top of the line Cadillac sedan. I loved my Mother very much, and it was my great joy to see her pleasure in this good fortune.

My wife, Muriel, got very restless in the meantime and kept pressing me to acquire my promised share of the business adding, "You can walk up Vine Street and do twice as well as you're doing with your Father. The time has come for you to stop being sentimental and improve our lot."

Although I felt disloyal to say it, I had to admit that my aim had been to give my Mother a better life and I had accomplished that. Now it did make sense for me to do the same for my own family.

I said to my Father, "You're working here for all these years. You've got a beautiful wife at home who would love to take a trip. You should take her to Miami. She was always talking about seeing Florida."

He said, "Now you're telling me what to do?"

I replied, "Listen. I'm your partner."

He said, "That's true." I never received any of the partnership. It was always numbers on a piece of paper. But I had never collected it. We always needed to have a balance to take care of the next thing. My parents went to Florida and had a wonderful time.

When they came back, I said to my Father, "Okay, you've had your trip. Now I want an accounting."

He argued, "An accounting of what?"

I declared, "An accounting of my 25% share."

"Is that the way to talk to a father?" he huffily complained.

I said, "My record speaks for itself. I'm happy that you have all the goodies. Now I think it's time that I should have some, too."

He said, "You see that door over there? When you came in, the door was open. When you leave, the door is going to be closed."

I asked, "You're firing me?"

He said, "No, I'm not firing you. I'm just telling you that if you keep that up, I don't want you around here."

Hurt at his attitude, I left and walked up Vine Street to the first office I passed, walked in and got a job as Philadelphia Sales Manager for Allied Artists Pictures earning $225.00 a week plus expenses. This began the painful cycle of me occasionally saving him financially. In addition, when he couldn't get movies from anybody, I would slip him some of mine. One of my great pleasures though, was that I had all new pictures to handle.

Our mainstay was the Bowery Boys series of crowd-pleasing feature films and also included titles such as DILLINGER and THE GANGSTER. At a general sales meeting in New York we were presented with a whole library of Hal Roach OUR GANG comedy shorts, which were re-titled, THE LITTLE RASCALS. The music to my ears was that every salesman would be entitled to a commission of 5% of all he could sell. In six months, I sold all of my screen possibilities and achieved a lifelong friendship with Steve Broidy, the President of the company.

My Mother died of leukemia on the eve of her fiftieth birthday. My Father fell apart completely, so I jumped in and made all of the funeral and burial arrangements. My grief was also overwhelming, but was lessened a bit in the knowledge that I had made her last years happier by helping provide her with the way of life to which I had always wanted her to be accustomed.

After about a year, I was contacted by Charles Conover, who started a new distribution company called Souvaine Selective Pictures. He invited me to join the company as Sales Manager for the Philadelphia, Pittsburgh, and Washington territories. My rate of pay was $300.00 a week plus expenses, against 10% of the gross collections. I lunged at it.

I launched and did publicity on Paul Gallo's film, NEVER TAKE NO FOR AN ANSWER, the story of St. Francis, patron saint of the animals.

One of the breaks I got was a spread in Life Magazine. Another release was the puppet version of CINDERELLA. I had a lot of fun beating Disney and his animated version to each city's premiere with my CINDERELLA.

While I was doing extremely well with my territory, the national experience was not measuring up. I was sad to see Souvaine fold its tent and disappear. What was I to do next?

I was besieged by offers from at least half of the studio's distribution departments. My Father came to me and offered me his parental wisdom saying, "Now that you've learned what it's all about, come on back to the family business and we'll split 50/50."

I told him we couldn't work together. Since he had previously bid me goodbye business-wise, I'd been able to move my family to a beautiful California ranch-style house in Broomall, Pennsylvania, and provide them with a much better lifestyle.

I told him that because I had my eye on the future, I would always remember the day he and I were crossing Broadway at 50th Street, and I looked up at the marquee of the Astor Theatre and said, "Someday there will be a Harris production on that marquee," and you told me to stop dreaming. "I can never stop dreaming. I do a lot of it, so I must decline your invitation."

He bitterly told me, "Well, you've done it again, so this time I'm quitting you. Just go on about your business and don't expect anything from me. Forget my telephone number."

I was extremely hurt by his attitude and resolved to someday bridge the gap. This was made difficult for me because friends were coming to me with stories about their conversations with my Father in which he accused me of leaving him high and dry, taking all of his contacts, which didn't exist, and trying to put him out of business. It was terribly embarrassing for me to hear these things.

My only response was "You know me. If you want to believe that crap, it's up to you."

I felt that I could never work for anyone again. I had to go with my heart. I opened my own office on Film Row in a second floor space above a taproom. My only display on Vine Street was the entrance door, which I painted fire engine red and mounted a futuristic looking white, free form board sign on it, which read, "Jack H. Harris Distributing Company." I had tasty furniture in my office, which consisted of a sofa and a beautiful desk and a posture chair for me. The anteroom housed my secretary.

One thing was missing, I had no pictures to distribute and my funds were drying up.

I contacted Max Rosenberg, a former attorney, who decided to go into producing independently. He was delighted to hear from me since he had just completed a forgettable movie called CHAINED FOR LIFE starring Daisy and Violet Hilton, the famous Siamese twins. The movie's theme centered on the enigma of one of the twins catching her husband cheating and then shooting him dead. She pled guilty at the trial, and the verdict was death. But, how could she be executed when her innocent twin would also die?

What made it interesting was that besides negotiating the playdates for the film, I could also deliver the twins in person to do their act and sell photos and autographs to supplement their share of the proceeds.

One sister was sweet and charming, her twin was a world-class bitch who was never satisfied with anything that I, or the theatre people, did for them. But, we got through this unique combination of Vaudeville and movies. Most of our exhibition points were drive-in theatres, which normally didn't have any live attractions.

I worked for thirty days lining up the tour and managing all of the details. Within three months, the whole thing was over. I had myself a $20,000 stake after expenses, which enabled me to continue on acquiring new, meaningful releases.

Charles Casanave, the aforementioned head man for David O' Selznick's reissue program, called me one morning to announce that he was in a deal to franchise Fred Astaire Dance Studios, in various key cities in the United States. The first studio was already in motion in New York City and running successfully. He remembered the magnificent publicity campaign I did on TOM SAWYER and wondered if I was interested in publicizing Fred Astaire Dance Studios of Philadelphia.

I accepted the assignment since it could be accomplished along with my distribution chores. Over a two-year period, I publicized the studio and soon created a local ABC-TV half hour featuring the kiddie dancing school section of the studio. I wrote, produced, directed and my eight-year-old daughter, Lynda, dramatized all the commercials. We both had a great time. However, my own business now required a full time commitment, forcing me to resign from this fun experience.

While I was on tour with the Hilton twins, I got an emergency call from Ted Minsky, head film buyer for the Warner Brothers Theatre circuit, which then dominated Eastern Pennsylvania and South Jersey. He wanted me to go to Cleveland, Ohio and meet with an exhibitor named Vance Schwartz, because he had a movie to distribute that would make me a millionaire. I got back to my office and determined that my round trip to Ohio would cost 250 sorely needed dollars and deprive me of an opportunity to pay attention to my business.

I called Vance and told him that he would have to come to me because I couldn't get away. He had a movie titled BOB AND SALLY that was produced by Universal Pictures, who had elected not to distribute the film. The movie told the story of a couple trying to get pregnant and how they overcame obstacles to make that happen. The birth scene was photographed in an actual delivery room with nurses and doctors in full attendance, and the baby emerging from a woman's vagina. This sounds pretty tame today, but in 1950 there were many territories that had censor boards. The Pennsylvania Board of Censors was one of them, which meant that every movie had to have a censor seal to be exhibited in Pennsylvania.

The Chairman of the Pennsylvania Board of Censors, Edna R. Carroll, happened to be my adoptive godmother. I went to her with a plea that it would mean a lot to my family if she would put the seal of approval on this picture because, "After all, childbirth is a precious thing and under the right auspices can be shown to segregated audiences to enlighten them."

We took the week and divided it up into three days for men and four days for women. There was a sex book that was offered for sale at each performance. She agreed to give us a license because the quality of the movie was not exploitative, and the production was really first class. She also did it for me.

What I received was a license to make money. I quickly learned the spiel enticing the audience to purchase the books and, with the help of the ushers in the various theatres, we sold them by the case. I got the theatres to charge an advance admission going from fifty cents to a dollar, and they paid me 50%. They were literally getting the picture for free, since they didn't have to pay any film rental out of their share. The book sales usually grossed as much as the film rental. I learned how you could make $1,000 a day in the distribution business without a big overhead.

The picture was endorsed by every school, government, and religious body except the Catholic Church, so we avoided the Catholic neighborhoods. The women's shows out grossed the men's. The only faints we ever had were during the men's shows where some of these big truck driver patrons would just faint at the sight of the birth.

Within weeks of the start of exhibition of BOB AND SALLY, Max Rosenberg came to me with a birth of a baby movie he had made called BECAUSE OF EVE. Now I had two birthing movies to offer. There soon was one additional birthing movie called MOM AND DAD. Although I had paved its way for a Censor Seal, I didn't get that one. It went to one of my competitors and we soon found out whichever "birth" movie came to a town first would do all the business. You don't have to guess who got to the towns first. I acquired a dozen small movies which were used as fillers and second features.

I was in Los Angeles for a few days, and while checking in by phone with the family, I heard my son, Anthony, clamoring to get to talk to me. I said to Muriel, "For Christ's sake, put him on. He never wants to talk to me."

He got on the phone and exclaimed, "Dad, Dad! I saw the most wonderful thing on the Disney television show last night. Davy Crockett – did you ever hear of him?"

Intrigued, I replied, "Tell me more."

He said, "He's got this great song, and I can't stop playing it on my guitar."

I told him I'd never heard of it, but I'd sure look into it.

"You'll be home by the time the next one's on and we'll watch it together," he said.

"You got that right."

I did a quick telephone survey among my exhibitor friends who all reported that their kids were nuts about Davy Crockett. Even my film buyer friends were Davy Crocket fans.

Very coincidentally, I was offered two reissue westerns. One was called IRIQUOIS TRAIL, and the second was called DAVY CROCKETT,

INDIAN SCOUT. I grabbed the distribution rights for $3,000 flat outright. We went to the first run Stanton Theatre in Philadelphia and built a barricade front, which obliterated the theatre's architecture. It looked like a wild west setting with huge pictures all over the place of George Montgomery sporting a coonskin cap and a Davy Crockett outfit.

The blowup photos of George Montgomery were actually from the movie IROQUOIS TRAIL, because in DAVY CROCKET INDIAN SCOUT, he dressed in the standard Western outfit including a ten-gallon hat. The families must have been happy anyway, because they showed up in droves.

I made a tie-in with Capitol Records to give each kid a record of the title song from Disney's TV trilogy, DAVY CROCKETT, KING OF THE WILD FRONTIER. At subsidiary showings, and there were many, it was TOM SAWYER all over again in spades with newspaper sponsorship and retail store backup offering prizes and hoopla for the winner of the contest to find the best Davy Crockett impersonator.

Score one for my son, Anthony, for getting us the early tip-off on DAVY CROCKETT.

The promotion ran about six months and netted close to $100,000.00. The run was ended by Disney himself, deciding to exhibit the third TV episode in theatres. Our party was over except for normal subsidiary theatrical reissue showings.

The big studios were in a state of flux, and their film libraries were being offered to independent distributors. The studios realized that their older pictures were sitting in the warehouse, because their distribution staffs were busy with current releases. Television exposure had yet to materialize, so they offered reissue rights for their inactive film libraries to independent distributors. I was quick to act and acquired all the Samuel Goldwyn titles, all of the Howard Hughes titles from his RKO Studios, and Warner Brothers' titles for my territory.

In combing the records, I came upon a 1928 Warner Brothers feature written by Darryl F. Zanuck called NOAH'S ARK. I set up the very first 100-theatre premiere throughout my Pennsylvania territory, backed by then unheard of full color ads in the Philadelphia Inquirer. Cecille B.

DeMille's THE TEN COMMANDMENTS was getting double advance admission and showing in theatres that had to be 100 miles apart. I offered patrons THE BIBLE in their own neighborhood at regular prices and succeeded handsomely.

I tried the "hundred theatre" premiere strategy again with Warner Brothers. YANKEE DOODLE DANDY starring James Cagney and got the screens, but only mild patronage.

I had a lot of fun with KING KONG and SON OF KONG as a double bill, and various other monster movies. One rainy night, THE THING, my reissue, was playing two miles from my home. Since I'd never seen it, I went to the theatre that night and saw this wonderful classic that would inspire me in the future.

I was distributing titles such as BEAST WITH A MILLION EYES and KING DINOSAUR with a massive TV campaign. It was backed by TV trailers which gave me the unusual experience of playing in a bunch of third tier theatres, doing so well that first and second tier theatres picked the same movies up right afterwards and repeated the success. My company was thriving, now with twelve very busy employees, four in the booking department alone. My release list included over 700 titles, some new, some old, some evergreen.

Two years and many unanswered phone calls had gone by since my last conversation with my Dad. He had stopped talking to me since I was out working on my own and had achieved a meaningful degree of success. I was always the first person to get to my office in the morning. One morning, at about 8:00 AM, I answered the phone and it was my Father.

He asked, "You know who this is?"

I responded, "I think so."

He went on, "I know you've called me a number of times. I was a jealous fool and didn't speak with you."

I inquired, "Well, what's on your mind?"

"Can you spare a few minutes to come over to my office and talk to me?" he asked. "I have something very serious to discuss with you."

He sounded troubled, I said unhesitatingly, "I'll be right there."

I walked into his office and he was sitting at a desk holding his head in his hands – on the verge of tears. I walked over to him and put my hand on his shoulder, "Come on, Dad, what's the trouble?"

He said, "I can't sleep, I'm so upset. I took a sleeping pill last night and your Mother came to me in a dream and said, 'Call Jack.'"

I was touched and could only say, "What's causing you so much difficulty?"

He answered, "I don't know how it happened, but I had an emergency and I needed the money and…"

"What money?"

He said, "Well, money belonging to producers for their share of the income."

I asked him if he tried to do some time payments with them.

He showed me documentation which revealed that he already owed the money that should have been paid on a current, weekly basis over eight months. He was facing court action. He owed $15,000 and had no cash, but he did have an elegant home loaded with antiques, artwork, and statuary. I knew what those things had meant to him and my late Mother. I went to his producers and made settlements with them and brought them up to date with payments. He promised to pay me little by little over the next year. While he never made good on his re-payment promise, I gained being able to talk to my Father again, along with the good feeling of helping his self-esteem by keeping him in business. I could tell more stories like that about my Father. But I'm sure it would get too exhausting for both me writing them and you reading them. For the entirety of my business life, however, any time a decision needed to be made, I would always try and do the opposite of my Father. In the meantime, I was anxious to break out of the neighborhood.

⌘

Chapter 8: The National Picture

At this point, USA theatrical motion picture distribution was accomplished by major studios providing pictures through their twenty-eight geographical branch offices. At the same time there were independent producing companies that franchised their product to independent distributors in each of the same twenty-eight geographical locations.

My company had expanded into the Washington D.C. and Pittsburgh, PA territories, thereby covering the surrounding geographical areas concerned. My time was divided between our three offices to allow me some hands on supervisory capability. Further, I had to make almost bi-weekly trips to New York to meet with my product suppliers. I was on the go from 7:00 AM to 9:00 PM on weekdays and highly valued my weekends, usually spent with my family, Muriel, Anthony, and Lynda.

Every Saturday the kids would wake me by 10:00 AM. They were dressed and ready for Daddy's Day Out, which allowed us to roam the historic and interesting highlights of Philadelphia, while Muriel had a welcome day to herself. The day would start with Anthony, Lynda, and me in the car discussing a program for the day from among several options: the zoo, the Franklin Institute, Independence Hall, Betsy Ross's house, the Liberty Bell, and the Philadelphia Museum of Art, later made famous by its appearance in the film ROCKY, where Sylvester Stallone would train by running up and down the endless steps to the entrance. We also enjoyed sporting events and live theatre whenever possible.

Lynda was cuter than cute, had a natural gift of gab and a most compelling nature. Anthony was handsome, athletic, and laid-back. I look back on these Saturdays with nostalgia and love. Much to Anthony's good-natured chagrin, we spent an inordinate amount of time at the art museum. I'd had a formal training in art and still dabbled with it in the preparation of press books and advertising materials for film releases. Lynda had a budding artist's sense and was truly enraptured with absorbing the art works at this famous institution. Sundays were family days, where we all relaxed and enjoyed our home together.

In 1952, I bought out Screen Guild, a larger competitor of mine in the Philadelphia Film Exchange territory. I merged my program with theirs

Daddy's Day with Muriel, Anthony and Lynda, 1950.

and conducted business. This left our current office space vacant. Walt Disney was expanding into national distribution and leased my former business quarters. It was nice to be Disney's Philadelphia landlord. Now their national organization was staffed with people I knew. During a meeting in their New York headquarters I was offered ETERNAL CITY, a Disney documentary about the Vatican and the Michaelangelo artwork. The Disney organization couldn't figure out what to do with it, feeling that perhaps I could find some theatre screens that would be graced by ETERNAL CITY.

My brainstorm was to enlist the church in the promo for the exhibition of ETERNAL CITY. I held a screening for Archbishop Frank O'Hara and his staff of the Philadelphia Diocese. Applause at the end of the screening showed their enjoyment of the picture.

To enlist their support, I recalled my theatre management experience in the late 1930s when I was invited to a Catholic Church sermon that listed the then condemned movies. The priest solicited an oath from the parishioners that they would not attend a condemned movie, or even patronize a theatre that had shown one. I studiously avoided condemned movies in my theatres. Now I was giving the Catholic Church the opportunity to not condemn, but to support a wonderful movie about the Holy See. I envisioned hordes of kids and their Sisters (teachers) being bussed to the movie at reduced rates to be engrossed and entertained by one of the finest feature films that recorded the history of their faith. The adults would also be able to see the movie at a discount. These discounts were in lieu of our donation to the Diocese. Upon me pitching them this idea, they heartily agreed and began selling discount movie tickets at each Catholic Church.

I booked ETERNAL CITY into the 400 seat Europa Theatre on Market Street in Philadelphia. During the first six weeks the attendance was so huge each local Catholic Church had to make advance-seating reservations. Disney had their distribution plan and the Diocese was able to support a worthy film. This made for a true success.

When the engagement was concluded, I was notified that Archbishop O'Hara was coming to my office to see me. At the appointed hour I was in my private office finishing a long distance telephone call. I could faintly hear the arrival of the church group at our entrance hall. There was some talking and then silence. I then heard the front door slam shut. I rushed to the lobby to greet the Archbishop and encountered only my secretary standing there, looking dejected. She explained that the holy man and his minions said something about a condemned movie poster and left in a huff.

I glanced around at the posters decorating the entrance hall and noticed a new one, THE MOON IS BLUE. I asked my sales manager where it came from, and he explained it was put there by Elmer Hollander, sales rep of United Artist, to whom I had rented a small office on our premises. He handled a few releases that were selected by United Artists for special treatment away from their office up the street.

THE MOON IS BLUE, directed by Otto Preminger, starring William Holden, David Niven and Maggie MacNamara, was a delightful story of two older playboys vying for the attentions of a youthful beauty. It was also condemned by the Legion of Decency.

The Archbishop had intended to present me with a commendation for my part in bringing ETERNAL CITY to their attention. He withdrew when he saw the poster for THE MOON IS BLUE. I tried calling him to no avail. I did give an explanation to his assistant of having no real business connection with THE MOON IS BLUE. He rewarded me with a front-page story in Variety complaining of my treachery after he and his staff went all out to support the Philadelphia premiere of ETERNAL CITY. The Industry knows the truth, so I was unhurt by the derogatory story. At least they spelled my name right. An interesting post-script to this story is that THE MOON IS BLUE was the only one of many condemned movies to actually show a nice profit. The passage of years made the Legion of Decency less and less important. Gradually it merged into the rating system that is now in effect.

Robert L. Lippert, an exhibitor, rose to prominence by distress purchasing a group of California theatres that were owned by Japanese nationals who were sent to Federal Internment Camps during WWII. Robert operated the theatres most successfully and branched into film production in 1950. Lippert Productions were smaller films that were distributed by a group of independent franchise holders. I had the franchise for my territory

In 1953, Robert held a franchisee conference in Chicago to announce his slate of films for the 1954 season. As the drinks and hors d'oeuvres were being consumed, various franchise holders took the floor to extoll the creativity of Robert and his valuable program. He suddenly turned to me and asked, "Jack, what have you got to say?"

Replying easily, I just spoke my mind, "Bob, I think you're terrific, but your program stinks. Five no name black-and-white westerns and a British women's prison import. Don't look for any miracles from my territory."

Unprepared for this negative reply, Robert (playing to the crowd) asked, "Well, Mr. Expert, what kind of movies would you prefer?"

That was easy to answer, "A monster movie in color with a sensible plot."

Bob came back with, "Oh, a monster horse."

"No," I said, "An original monster. A real threat to mankind."

"Sounds great, Jack," he magnanimously replied. "Why don't you go out and make this world beater?"

I exclaimed, "I shall!"

By 1955, Robert had signed on at 20th Century Fox to supply a program of their minor films and was no longer a supplier for the independent distributors. While Robert was beginning his work for 20th Century Fox, I kept developing the idea for the movie that would become THE BLOB.

Early one Monday morning in 1953, I got a phone call from Michael Friedman. He was one of my New York mentors who owned a company called Comprehensive Service, whose mission it was to equip and supply motion picture developing and printing laboratories throughout the world. The funny and unique thing about meetings with Michael, was that to meet with him was also to take a meeting with his wife, Carmen, who had a bit of a big mouth. Michael would let her do some of the shouting, and then we'd meet privately to take care of business. After mutually knowing each other's work and respecting each other for some time, we had come to be friends and colleagues, and I was happy to place my films in the hands of his lab.

Michael knew that I had long been hard at work in the film industry, distributing and advertising other people's movies. We had also discussed my desire to make my own film, and my early concept for what became THE BLOB. In our third meeting, Michael said, "I've looked over your action more closely. You have to meet another client of mine." His other client was The Boy Scouts of America (BSA).

He knew that the Boy Scouts had made a movie called JAMBOREE, which was the story of the annual Boy Scout gathering that took place in various cities, that year in Hollywood. In a weird way, it might have been ahead of its time, as it was a documentary that partially dramatized these Boy Scout events. Of course, films experimenting with the notion of what is or isn't "documentary filmmaking" have become more mainstream in recent years, generating a lot of controversy while making a lot of money. At the time, JAMBOREE had been in editing for about three months. Cecil B. DeMille had helped set it up and some of the stars in it were Bob Hope, Danny Kaye, Jimmy Stewart, Alan Ladd, Lucille Ball, Betty Hutton, among many more celebrities. BSA owned it, and expected to distribute it.

Michael arranged for me to meet with Irvine H. Millgate, who was the Head of Visual and Audio for BSA, as well as being in charge of completion details of JAMBOREE. Irvines's day job was professor of Humanities at Northwestern University, Evanstone, Illinois. We went into a little screening room in Michael's suite and looked at the rough cut of the picture. It was seventy-five minutes long and told the simple story of how the Boy Scouts, told through the lens of one in particular, had to do chores and earn money to afford the round trip to attend the Jamboree. The vignettes of how the various scouts accomplished this chore really had heart, and the cameo performances of Hollywood's top stars didn't hurt its box office potential.

With all of this in mind, I was bowled over with the possibilities of exhibiting this film throughout the country. The Chief Scout Master of the BSA and his executives, including Irvine H. Millgate, met with me at the New York Athletic Club to discuss a deal naming me as national consultant for the distribution and exhibition of their feature film. They were not as interested in how much money they'd get, as they were in how many theatres would show the picture.

I outlined a plan to maximize this possibility and also earn them a tidy profit. The first proviso was that I could get the film in all the major markets, but that Millgate would be traveling there with me to promote every showing with the help of the local chapters of the BSA. My other plan was procuring another feature film to fill out the bill, as this was the day of double features.

A French company had completed a feature film starring Laurel and Hardy in which Stan Laurel inherits an island and Oliver Hardy is his legal counsel. Their plan is to establish a country with only qualified, good citizens, and no confiscatory laws or taxes. I went to Paris and viewed the picture. I saw an addled, uncertain Stan Laurel and a subdued Oliver Hardy. I was a fan of theirs since their accidental teaming in the silent days to their heyday at MGM. Clearly, this one was a far cry from their beloved, peak performances. Still, it was Laurel and Hardy in a new, almost good movie.

Henry Deutschmeister, a grizzled German, had moved to France and created a viable production/distribution company. He owned the picture. We haggled over the price and settled at $50,000 for all U.S. rights in perpetuity. I quickly bought the U.S. rights with co-financing by Michael Friedman. We became partners in the enterprise. I called the movie, LAUREL AND HARDY IN UTOPIA. I knew that Laurel and Hardy had not worked as a team in almost fifteen years. The main reason for this was that sadly, the world had moved on from the famous duo. I also knew that my competition for acquiring the picture was almost none. The major studios had no interest in it, and most of the independents were either unaware of it or didn't care about it. I had my work cut out for me, but I figured JAMBOREE could use the entertainment help, and LAUREL AND HARDY IN UTOPIA could be a good backup to the attention that JAMBOREE would generate.

It was screened for the BSA brass, and they eagerly accepted it as a companion for their picture, provided we would change one scene where Laurel and Hardy share a bottle of wine. This was a bad example for the Boy Scouts. I did an insert close-up of my hand holding a bottle labeled grape juice, and that solved the problem.

Irvine and I traveled the U.S. including stops in New York, Milwaukee, Los Angeles, Chicago, and Boston in order to convene the local Boy Scout troops and, together with our franchises, work out campaign plans for each of the territories concerned. The campaign included twenty-four sheet posters, discount tickets sold by Boy Scouts to their families and friends, and other media events in each of the territories.

We opened JAMBOREE in Boston with a rousing campaign and a ninety theatre premiere. Our franchisee, Joseph E. Levine, who later became famous as a national producer/distributor for 300 films of major note, was in love with the picture but chose not to show LAUREL AND HARDY IN UTOPIA with it.

The Boy Scouts were thrilled with the exposure. This was how a movie that nobody else knew how to distribute or promote became a minor hit. I was disappointed that my other picture wasn't shown. The Boston experience spread through the country and LAUREL AND HARDY IN UTOPIA stayed in the can. Leading executives of the then National Council of the Boy Scouts of America were so pleased with the JAMBOREE experience that they made me a member of their council.

The Millgate/Harris tour lasted about six months. When the speeches and crowd inducing rhetoric ceased for the day, we'd sit down to a quiet supper and talk about family and other things. At most of these supper meetings Irvine would tell me how proud he was to be associated with me and my showbusiness acumen. I was equally grateful for our association.

One night, Irvine asked me, "What's your next project?"

I replied, "Well, I've got a routine western and a -"

He interrupted me, "When are you going to start making your own movies?"

I wondered aloud, "How do you know I can make a movie?"

Assuredly he answered, "You can make a movie. And you can make a hell of a movie." It was very encouraging.

Then Irvine proposed a question, "If you could make a movie, Jack, you certainly wouldn't have to worry about distribution. But what would you envision as the content?"

"That's easy, Irv," I replied. "It would have to be science fiction, and in color. I would want to get two or three times the budget of these little black and white twofers that consist of a title and a poster and very little else. The monster would have to be one never conceived of before. A menace to people that was literally indestructible. Something that if not arrested or destroyed would envelop the earth. Yet able to be done in by something Grandma could cook up on her kitchen stove."

Irvine said, "That's pretty damn good." Then the conversation would go off to what kind of a monster it would be. We would jot the highlights on our writing pads, and as we were saying goodnight to each other we agreed we didn't have it yet.

As the idea that would become THE BLOB was in its earliest stages, and with JAMBOREE a success in its own right, I found myself stuck holding onto LAUREL AND HARDY IN UTOPIA. Michael Friedman called me one day wanting to know what we were going to do with the picture. For want of a better answer I replied, "I'm working on an idea."

One Sunday, my wife and kids and I went to our country club for dinner. While we were waiting to be seated, we watched an episode of Ralph Edwards, "This Is Your Life," running on a TV in the lobby. The kick of it was always to try and guess whose life would be honored that night. To my astonishment, Ralph said, "This is your life, Oliver Hardy."

We sat glued to the set and watched the entire show where first Stan Laurel and then Oliver Hardy were surprised and honored at what they thought was going to be a local television interview, but turned out to be one of the hottest shows of that vintage. We went into the dining room and I was walking on air as Muriel and I were sipping our cocktails, she said, "What are you going to do about it?"

I replied, "There couldn't be a better break. Believe me I'll be on the horn first thing tomorrow with some major New York circuits." I knew this was possibly wishful thinking, because I had tried all the circuits before to get the picture started. This time, I believed I could get the picture off the ground and into the theatres tomorrow due to this exposure.

At 7:30 AM the following day, I went into my office and surrounded myself with artwork from the press book and posters on LAUREL AND HARDY IN UTOPIA. I didn't have a clue as to how to parlay the exposure from the Ralph Edwards TV show to exhibition in important theatres. I went through some routine matters hoping for a clue, when about 9:45 AM, my secretary called me to say that Marty Polin was on the phone from New York. He was the head buyer for what was then RKO Theatres, the dominant theatre circuit in New York City, if not the USA. After exchanging pleasantries, he said, "What are you doing with that Laurel and Hardy piece of crap?"

I said, "It's hanging on my wall like a fine oil painting. I better get off my butt and get it in some theatres."

He said, "Why do you think I'm calling you?"

I answered, "I don't know."

He said, "We're stuck for a picture in two weeks. What would you say if we booked it into The Palace on Broadway first run, then followed with a circuit spread of fifty houses over the next month or so?"

I took a deep breath and replied, "It sounds interesting, but how much do we get for granting you this privilege?"

"Think it over and call me in an hour with your price."

I used the hour as sensibly as I could, knowing full well that I had to make this deal. I contacted various buddies in New York to get a line on what the booking was worth. I came to the conclusion that anything from $20,000 up would be acceptable.

I called Marty back on the appointed hour and told him I had to have $40,000.

He pointed out, "It's only worth $20,000, but we're stuck for a picture. So, how soon can we get the prints?"

With that deal in the can, moving LAUREL AND HARDY IN UTOPIA throughout the country went from impossible to easy. Bless Ralph Edwards.

I made a trip to Hollywood to set up a Los Angeles premiere of the Laurel and Hardy movie. While there, I invited my two stars to lunch in Santa Monica. I was embarrassed to arrive at the restaurant over one hour late because I had made a wrong turn and wound up in Downtown L.A. I had to zip back to Santa Monica to meet them.

Oliver was all smiles and Stan was pleasant. They quickly expressed their gratitude for the opportunity to meet the guy that made their picture available to the American audiences. They regaled me with stories about their experience ahead of *This is Your Life.* Oliver told me that he would walk into the house and notice his wife would get off the phone quickly to greet him. The first time this happened he thought, "How nice." The fifth time it happened, he got suspicious.

One day he came home a little early from a golf game and although her car was there, he couldn't find her. He did locate her up in the attic, which she hadn't stepped foot into for ten years. She just explained she was looking for an old party invitation, and she didn't want to bother him about it.

That evening the phone rang. She ran to answer it in another room, and was much muffled with her conversation. He walked into the other room and she abruptly hung up the telephone. He thought, "Well, after all these years of marriage, she found a lover." All of her mysterious actions were self-explanatory after his appearance on the show. She had been the source of the Oliver Hardy History Research.

Oliver passed away within eighteen months of our meeting, and Stan retired into an assisted living location, passing away in 1965. Spending that couple of hours with them was among my fondest memories and made me thankful to be part of this industry where I had the good fortune to realize my wildest dreams. I get a glow remembering sharing that moment with my idols.

⌘

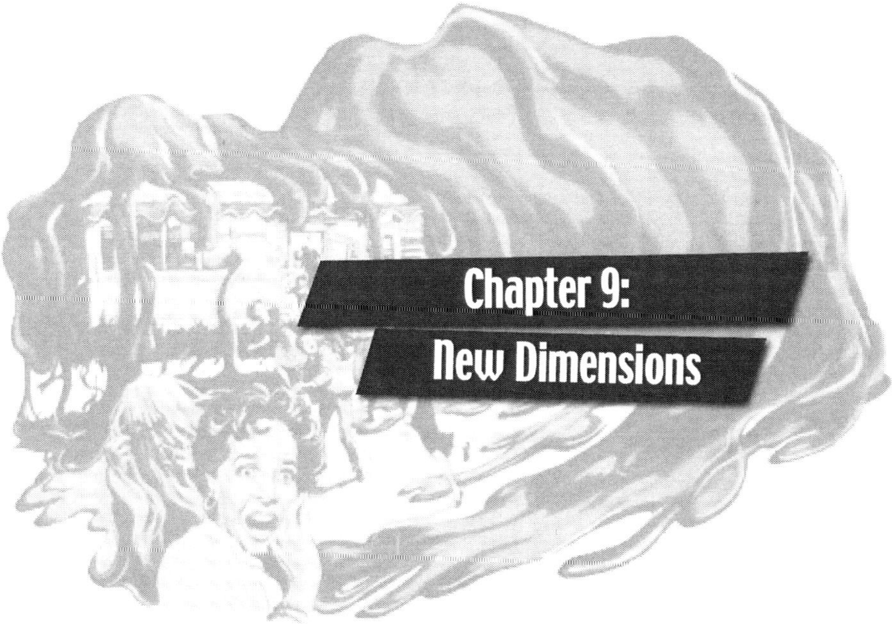

Chapter 9: New Dimensions

One of the questions I get asked about THE BLOB and the following films I made was whether or not I felt comfortable with them being referred to as "B-movies" or "Cult films." I feel that these films all fit into one clearly-defined genre – scary movies. If THE BLOB taught me anything, it's that if you can make a good scary movie, then you can make a fortune.

What made THE BLOB unique was that it was actually a teenage story. Up until then, the victims in monster movies were often faceless, less fully formed characters and stereotypes. The audience related to the characters in the BLOB, particularly Steve and Jane.

Scranton, Pennsylvania was a middle-sized coal-mining town, and it was the place where two theatre circuits had their home offices. I left a meeting there to catch a train to New York, and stopped at a magazine stand to pick up something to read. I noticed a cover of a *Weird Tales Magazine*, which showed a man disappearing into a brick wall as he was escaping from something. It read, "*The Thrill of the 4th Dimension.*" I was fascinated and stopped to use the telephone to call Shorty and describe what I had seen.

He said, "Well, that's somebody going through a brick wall that has no entrance without getting bruised."

I said, "Yes."

He continued, "You know we're in the third dimension? That's length, breadth, and thickness."

I said, "This guy was going through the brick wall."

"That must be the fourth dimension," he observed.

He was excited. I said, "Good, excite your people."

I had to catch my train and promised to talk to him the next day.

I kept thinking about how we could build a movie around this 4th dimensional idea. The very benign title, THE 4D MAN, sort of wrote itself.

We knew that our protagonist had to be a monster. We came up with the idea of him using up his life span rapidly when he was in the 4th dimensional state. Although he could not replenish his life spark, he could stop his aging process by stealing the life spark from and killing other humans.

Shorty, Ted Simonson, and I had a few story conferences and came up with very little else. Si Chermak, a writer who had a couple of his scripts produced, became available and in one session told us his idea for the plot. He also told us, frankly, he needed money badly for a trip to California to see his cousin, who was the supervisor of all television at Universal Studios.

Shorty said, "We'll give you $500 if you deliver a finished screenplay within seven working days."

He quickly agreed and produced a very literate, shooting script to which we made no changes except one. I had seen Patty Duke on a segment of *$64,000 Question.* She was about twelve-years-old and looked eight. I was completely seduced by her personality and the romance the camera had with her facial expressions and her eyes. I said that we had to write her into the picture, and Patty Duke's debut in movies was via a small part in THE 4D MAN.

Casting was not as difficult as it was on THE BLOB, because lots of managers wanted their clients to be in our next picture. We had an option of Steve McQueen for additional pictures and decided not to exercise the option. We felt he was too much trouble. We lucked into Robert Lansing and James Congdon from Broadway, and got a bright idea to use former Miss America and very famous *Good Morning America* weathergirl, Lee Merriweather, for our female lead. This gave us some name value in the bargain. Robert Strauss of STALAG 17 fame, (both on Broadway and in the movie) was cast to play the heavy. Shorty directed and Bart Sloan produced the special effects.

Lee Merriweather announced her marriage had taken place two days before we started shooting. The lucky man was Frank Aletter, a well-known stage actor. They had a short distance honeymoon, and marriage, consisting of weekends only, until we finished production about six weeks later in our now regular stomping grounds of Chester Springs, PA.

While we were in production, I got a call from Fred Coe requesting information on Patty Duke. He said she could be up for the lead in the stage production of "The Miracle Worker." I gave a rave review of her work for us, and sent a rough cut of her scenes to them for screening. She got the part, and later played the lead in the movie version, for which she won an Oscar for Best Actress in a Supporting Role. She went on to star in the *Patty Duke Show,* and to accumulate countless other movie and TV credits. I like to say that I discovered Patty Duke.

Years later, I walked into the Hamburger Hamlet on Sunset Blvd. in Beverly Hills. Right in the front booth was Patty Duke, red eyed and crying, being consoled by Lucie Arnaz. Patty called me over and I sat down and held her hand.

I inquired with her, "What is it, dear? What's so terrible?"

She stood up and showed me her enormous belly, explaining that Desi, Jr. was responsible, and that Lucie was trying to work out something to get her brother to take responsibility for the coming, blessed event.

Months later the baby was born and although she didn't need the money, Desi made some financial commitments for the child's support.

Production proved very exacting because once again, after we finished our six-week shooting phase, it took close to four months to complete all of the special effects. We wound up a bit over budget, at a cost just shy of $150,000. I had made the picture independently and put up the entire budget without a distribution deal. I believed that Paramount should be hungry for it considering their outstanding success with THE BLOB, but to my great disappointment, Paramount, Fox, Warner Brothers, Columbia, and MGM all turned the picture down.

Some producers would panic at this turn of events, but in my back pocket, I had years of exhibition and distribution experience that made me unafraid to handle it myself.

Max Youngstein, President of United Artists, raved about the picture, telling me it was the most literate science fiction picture he had ever seen. But, he had no place for it in his schedule. Steve Broidy, my old boss at Allied Artists, offered to distribute the picture if I would accept $75,000 as a minimum guarantee. I told him I couldn't afford it.

He said, 'Well, you've got that. If you can better the offer elsewhere, good luck to you."

In the meantime, promotion had to go on. We took out a policy from Lloyds of London that would pay one million dollars to anyone who could duplicate in real life the feats of the 4D Man in our picture. It made for good publicity. Even until today, nobody has come forth to claim the prize.

I had made the acquaintance of Hy Martin, then president of Universal Pictures when I was distributing their picture, BOB AND SALLY. I asked him to look at 4D MAN and held my breath.

He screened it, and we met in his office on Park Ave. in New York. I told him I wanted $200,000 in front as a minimum guarantee. He asked me how much the picture cost. In a nice way, I responded, "None of your god damned business."

He said, "Let me see what we can do."

We met the following week and were having tea in his office when he said, "Jack, I personally love your picture. I think we can certainly say, 'From the producer of THE BLOB, in all the advertising.'"

I said, "It might not help, but it couldn't hurt."

He went on, "Now as far as the advance is concerned, we can't give you one, but if you cast your lot with us, I promise you a wonderful job of distribution."

People have said to me that I register my emotions very clearly with my eyes and face. I must have looked grief stricken because Hy started to laugh and reached into a special drawer, from which he pulled a ruled pad and he showed it to me. I read the only thing on the page that said, "$150,000."

Hy came over and hugged me and said, "Thanks for brightening up my otherwise gloomy day."

The deal was that they paid me $150,000 as an advance guarantee against a 50/50 split of profits, after Universal recouped its investment and the cost of prints, advertising, and its distribution fee. It was a five year deal and I retained all rights, except first run theatrical distribution in the U.S. and Canada only. In one fell swoop, I had covered the cost of production and had the rest of the world free for additional income. I made a deal with Wolfe Cohen, president of Warner Brothers International Distribution, to handle the picture in the rest of the world. I didn't need an advance at that point, because Warner Brothers is a major label in the foreign territories. I was happy to give them a 25% distribution fee, and not have to split any of the profits with them. The Warner Brothers deal ultimately brought me an extra $300,000.

Universal decided to premiere the picture in the Southeast, and lined up a three-week tour for Lee Merriweather and myself to promote the picture. We did a sterling job being ferried from radio station to TV station to chambers of commerce dinners, and wound up one day at an Atlanta TV station wherein the host of the program had been delayed by an auto accident. Lee Merriweather and I interviewed each other and praised the picture for the half hour of the show. We were the show except for commercials.

Scientist explains searching for the 4th Dimension in Philadelphia observatory to Lee Meriwether (Left) and Jack (Right).

We had one digression on our personal appearance tour to deliver the print of the picture to the first run theatre in Detroit, Michigan. We picked up the print just past the Canadian side of Niagara Falls. An Air National Guard Plexiglas-domed helicopter airlifted us. As we were in the air going over the falls Lee asked the pilot, "Have you ever flown under the falls?"

He was so smitten with her, he turned the craft back, and we had the thrill of a lifetime in flying under the falls with a left turn at the end towards Detroit. We made all the newspapers, and the stunt impressed even us.

This was the last stop on our tour. On our way back to L.A., Lee sat with me and read a newspaper. I took out an early script for my next possible feature. She saw what I was doing and asked, "Is there a part in it for my husband?"

4D MAN grossed over $4 million, a nice profit on a $150,000 film.

I had always been fascinated with dinosaurs, and decided since our crew was so facile with special effects that we should make a dinosaur film. During the shooting of 4D MAN, I became aware of Alfie Bestor, well-known writer for "Holiday Magazine," and author of several books, the rights to which had been purchased by two major studios. We sat down in my suite at the St. Regis Hotel in New York to iron out a plotline for a dinosaur movie, which I expected him to write. Instead of that, we brainstormed for three hours and came up with the framework of a plot: A construction crew is blasting the shoreline of a sparsely populated island in the Pacific, to create a harbor and foundation for a multi-million dollar resort complex. A couple of their explosive charges bring up two huge frozen masses from the very deep ocean floor. Each mass contains a fully formed dinosaur, which when left on the beach to thaw, would allow them to awake from their frozen sleep. That would give us prehistoric beasts and a contemporary jungle setting with modern man, which felt like a very good start.

When I proposed our next writing step to Alfie, he said, "You have your basic plot, go get a good writer. I have a very full plate and couldn't get to it for a couple of years."

I said Alfie, "What can I do for you? This has been wonderful of you."

He said, "You provided me with the proper booze and snacks, and it's been a pleasure to knock heads with you. I loved THE BLOB, and I was dying to meet you anyhow."

I said "Thank you."

He ended it with, "God Bless." We shook hands at the door and that's the last we saw of each other.

I hired famous sci-fi writer, Algis Budrys, and well-known Playhouse 90 script editor, Al Forman, to come to my home in Penn Valley, Pennsylvania to work with me and come up with a screenplay for the movie now called, DINOSAURUS. Muriel went to stay with her parents in Baltimore, and Lynda and Anthony were already at summer camp in the Pennsylvania highlands.

The writer's job was to write, and Al's job was to instruct him on the form to use for a screenplay. With the wife and kids gone, little did I know what was in store for me.

Al Forman, the editor, was a ten-to-sixer, which is the kind of schedule he kept at CBS. Budrys, the writer, was an insomniac, who pounded the typewriter all night long. When he went to sleep between 10:00 AM and Noon, we'd have a chance to read his work and make notes. This went on for five days and there was progress, but the volume of pages were unbelievable. There were 200 pages to go through and only 25% of the story told.

The editor came to me on the sixth day and said, "Jack, I'm taking your money for nothing. That guy is writing the script of a lifetime. I've never in my life had to proof read 200 pages by the fifth day of operation. When he's finished, if you need me, call me. We'll see if we can battle it into the proper length."

I bid him "adieu," and assumed my supervisory chores with the writer, who continued his twenty two hour a day schedule. 150 pages later, I got an emergency call from the summer camp my kids were attending to tell me that my son sustained a mishap on the playing field during a baseball game, the ball hit him smack in the eye. He needed emergency attention. Algys was sitting with me when I got the call. He stood up and said, "We have no time to go get transportation. You sit still. I'll go and get him. I know where the camp is."

I tried to hold him back. He just threw me off, jumped in his car and sped away. Alone in the house, I called our doctor who then made arrangements for hospitalization and an eye specialist to be on hand within two hours. I then called Muriel and told her that her Baltimore vacation was over and to come back home.

It seemed that I had just hung up the phone when the writer's car steamed into our driveway. Anthony was lying in the back, holding his eye with compresses. It was so swollen it looked like he had an extra head. He was running a temperature. I got in the car, and we sped to the hospital. The eye doctor was right there. Eight days later, my son emerged from the hospital with the necessity for another couple of weeks of attention promising complete recovery down the line.

Algys and I decided we had done whatever we could to beef up the screenplay, which was now almost 500 pages. He elected to go back home to New York to complete it and be ready for our next meeting.

I had presented the basic notion of DINOSAURUS to Hy Martin, President of Universal Pictures, he was totally blown away by the box office results of THE BLOB, and was pleasantly contented with the grossing ability of 4D MAN, which was not the sensation that THE BLOB had turned out to be. He wanted DINOSAURUS, and we put together a basic deal based upon his reading the screenplay. I told him what I was going through getting it put on paper. He said, "Jack, I'm a speed reader, and I love to read. No matter how many pages it is, get it to me so we can conclude a deal." He regretted not getting the rights to THE BLOB, and wasn't going to let DINOSAURUS go to another company.

I was shocked when I next met with Algys, who presented me with what looked like a telephone directory of 640 pages. The script noted the plot in microscopic detail. It was accompanied by a ten page précis discussing how the music should be written, how the various themes for the different characters should play, and what the title music should deliver.

I am not known to be easily rattled, but I had to take a deep breath and think it over carefully before I presented this document to Hy Martin. Timing is everything in this business. I bit the bullet, and delivered it to him.

Three days later, he summoned me to New York to discuss the matter of production. He knew that we'd be looking at a six-hour movie with the ensuing costs. I said, "This is not my first movie and this is not the final screenplay. It's a textbook on what elements the script should contain. I will deliver an eighty to ninety-minute picture, with full responsibility for all costs exceeding the $250,000 dollars that your company will put up as your part of the production cost. In return for that, I would own the negative and all rights excepting first theatrical distribution, and I will get the picture back in five years."

Hy Martin agreed, provided their distribution fee would be 25% and they would advance all prints and advertising, and then share with me 50/50 on the net proceeds.

I took the massive manuscript and worked out a writing arrangement with Dan Weisburd in Hollywood. We worked together to create a 120-page screenplay, which would be good enough to start a production breakdown. I had made a deal with the St. Croix Hotel in the Virgin Islands, who assured me that they would cover all location expenses provided I shot the movie on the island of St. Croix, an irresistible reason to have done so.

Shorty met me at St. Croix and we carefully examined the location and the accommodations, which were first class. The island had probably 150 tons of construction equipment including earthmovers, diggers, and dump trucks, as the island was under major development. We were allowed to use all of that in the movie gratis.

Shorty was quite impressed and agreed to direct the picture, provided I allow him and his wife, Jean, to do the director's breakdown on the screenplay. This was our first and last collaboration away from Chester Springs, Pennsylvania. We had decided that two weeks of location shooting would be followed by three weeks of interior and exterior studio shooting in Hollywood.

⌘

Jack H. Harris official publicity shot for Universal Pictures 4D Man and Dinosaurus, 1970.

Chapter 10: Hello Hollywood

On March 7, 1959, I opened the front door of my home in Penn Valley, Pennsylvania to find four feet of snow, which prevented me from going to the subterranean garage to get my car. There had been a crippling blizzard the night before, the severity of which was a total surprise. We eventually had no power and impassable streets, plus the California-style patio cover we had so carefully and expensively installed, was caved in like a demolition ball had landed on it. The street workers came through, eventually, with snow moving equipment and we were ferried to the home of my sister, Mitzie, who lived in a nearby neighborhood that was not affected as severely as we were. We camped out with Mitzie, her husband, and their four children.

We had a great time. I loved the kids and they loved Uncle Jack. My own teenaged kids could think of a dozen things they'd rather do than share such a crowded house.

The weather let up, the streets were usable, and power was restored. I sat down with Muriel and told her, "This is our last winter of glorious weather in Philadelphia. We're moving to sunny California as soon as it is practical."

Five foot tall ball of fire, Lynda, was deeply involved in her high school activities, couldn't imagine anything worse than having to move to the west coast at this stage of her life. Lynda and I talked it over. I told her we'd be making movies and be in the center of the industry that I'd spent my life in from a distance. Now we'd be in the thick of it. She was a ham, just like me, and quickly saw the merit in a change of venue.

Anthony, now a strapping 6'3" fifteen-year-old, had become an expert guitarist with a following of six students, including two adults, which he was teaching. He became morose and seriously depressed. It was rare to get a smile out of him. Muriel didn't like show business and didn't want to be taken to Hollywoodland, away from all of her friends and associates. She had become an interior designer and relished her resources and her clients.

I was adamant and had a great ally in my darling daughter. We overwhelmed the opposition. Now my lifelong dream of living in the heart of Hollywood with my own production company already established could be realized. As prophetic as Pete Smith was in 1940, Hollywood didn't send for me. It sort of forced me to go there, and at least it was on my own terms.

In early April 1959, I did some traveling to other parts of the U.S. to help promote the current distribution of 4D MAN. I wound up in Los Angeles and about a month later, I was joined there by Muriel, Anthony, and Lynda on what we called an exploratory trip. We were ensconced in the Presidential Suite of the Hollywood Roosevelt Hotel. Muriel and the kids were chauffeured about by studio limos to introduce them to the geography of the area, with a concentration on Beverly Hills as an ultimate home site.

After a week or so, we rented a car and drove out to Palm Springs for the weekend, where I got my first taste of the Southern California freeway system. In my distribution career, I had traveled by car on an average of 800 miles a week visiting theatre operators in Pennsylvania, New Jersey, and Delaware. After seven years of that, I had sworn off long distance driving. There we were, bumper-to-bumper from L.A. to Palm Springs, and the return trip was just as bad with the additional inconvenience of a sand storm thrown in just outside of Palm Springs. The round trip to Palm Springs indelibly impressed me with the need to avoid such trips in the future.

We had rented a three-bedroom condominium in Brentwood for six months pending the finding of our new abode. One morning I was sitting near the window overlooking the playground next to our apartment building when a lady came up to the window and asked permission to rest her coffee cup on our window sill. It was a youthful Angela Lansbury, there to watch her two youngsters playing tennis. She was charming and neighborly. Her kids were good athletes. A few days later, I told her that I had distributed an independent movie she made while I was living in Philadelphia. Angela was duly impressed since she felt it was a potboiler tossed off during one of her acting layoffs. It was nice to have spent coffee time with her. She went on to a brilliant career heading up many stage, screen, and television hits.

I was busy every minute in DINOSAURUS pre-production. I found Willis O'Brien, the special effects director of the original KING KONG, who, although he was near ninety-years-old, fell in love with my project and agreed to be consultant. He led us to a number of special effects geniuses. We settled on Project Unlimited, headed by Tim Barr, who could make a figurine come to life in any form we needed by virtue of stop motion photography. The other artists included Wah Chang, a famous designer of puppets and background paintings, and Gene Warren, who I liked immediately because he took me for a special effects meeting in his vintage Ford Thunderbird. The remarkable crew, along with Willis, became our special effects team.

Maurice Delgado, who had done most of the important brass skeletons for the stop motion puppeteers, turned out two stainless steel armature operated figures that brought our Tyrannosaurus Rex and Brontosaurus to vivid life. We designed all of the action sequences in specific detail to enable us to blend the normal motion shooting of the live actors seamlessly. This is how KING KONG was originally planned in 1931, and we were the first production to use this system since. Between KING KONG and DINOSAURUS, dinosaurs were created for the screen by animation cells, lizards with false appendages, puppets that were put into restricted motion by out of frame operators, and actors wearing dinosaur suits, such as GODZILLA (which I handled during my distribution days).

There was a model by the name of John Sutphen, who appeared in the Viceroy Cigarette television commercials. He had young Gary Cooper looks and a shock of thick, prematurely gray hair. The way he inhaled and exhaled the cigarette smoke boosted their sales tremendously. Although the public didn't know his name, they sure remembered that craggy, handsome face. We looked for him and were greatly surprised to learn that he had just been signed to a seven-year deal at Universal Studios, with a list of great titles and outstanding star ladies to play opposite, including Lana Turner, Doris Day and Loretta Young.

He had been sitting around for months waiting for his first screen assignment when I made a call to Hy Martin in New York, who was delighted to lend him to us as the star of the movie. He warned me that the studio had already renamed him, Ward Ramsey. I said we could live with it, provided we would pay the studio guild minimum for the duration of the shooting phase. They agreed.

We put out a casting call with the Screen Actors Guild (SAG) for our female lead and supporting players. I arrived at my office the next morning at 8:15 AM, and there were at least 100 actresses already there waiting to be interviewed. I assigned the job to Shorty and our production manager, Frank Parmenter. I quietly observed some of the auditions. It was hopeless.

As a courtesy, we selected about twenty of the ladies and dismissed the rest, and then we went to the Universal casting department for suggestions. They set us up with half a dozen hopefuls, and we selected the best two who had some recent experience that we could see on film. They seemed like they could do a good job.

I was of the unshakable opinion that the star of the show was really the dinosaurs. That is where we concentrated one-third of our $350,000 budget. We set up shop at Producers Studio, then being run by a great guy, Phil Krasne, who helped us assemble a good crew, set dressers, and production designers. We gave a copy of the DINOSAURUS script to Ron Stein, a talented composer, who wrote an outstanding musical score.

Back in my family life, I appointed Muriel to find us a house in Beverly Hills that did not require extensive alterations. Muriel found a Roman villa-style house under construction in the Trousdale Estates of Beverly Hills. Trousdale Estates was constructed on the former estate of the Doheny oil family, who then resided in Graystone Mansion. The individually designed and constructed residences had breath taking views encompassing the Sunset Strip and Beverly Hills lights at night, and a more pastoral view of the rolling hills of Coldwater Canyon to Bel Air in the daytime. All of Beverly Hills had been developed. This was the only opportunity to acquire a new house in Beverly Hills which met my parameters, of not wanting anything that we had to rebuild and customize. We were able to get it completed by the builder at a reasonable price. I should have foreseen that since Muriel had left a budding interior design career in Philadelphia, she would want additional things done to the house. I talked her into waiting for six months.

The day before we were frantically completing our preparation for the trip to the Virgin Islands, my secretary announced that Ward Ramsey was here to see me. I said, "Send him right in." I was on the phone when into my office stepped a handsome, tall, *black-haired* actor. I called my secretary and asked, "Where the hell is Ward Ramsey?"

She answered, "He's in your office, Mr. Harris." I didn't recognize him because his beautiful shock of premature gray hair that prompted us to hire him was dyed black. I bid him to have a seat. I got on the phone with Ed Mull, president of production at Universal Studios. I questioned him, "Ed, what the hell are you pulling on me?"

He replied, "What do you mean?"

I explained, "I hired a Gary Cooper type with premature white hair accenting his baby blue eyes. And two days before we start shooting you send me a guy who looks like he fell into a vat of black shoe polish."

Ed brushed me off with, "We had to do that to Cary Grant years ago, because everybody knows his hair is prematurely gray. I think he'll add an extra virility to your dinosaur thriller." In the interest of time and knowing the chances of bleaching going haywire, I decided to live with it.

I headed out to the Virgin Islands with my cast and crew to be ensconced at St. Croix and to get ready for shooting DINOSAURUS.

The first setback was that the promised location access by the hotel owners had failed to materialize. Now we had forty people sitting around. Thankfully, the only cost was their salaries, since room and board were being comped. We had to find a new, ocean-side location with plenty of over and under growth, along with suitable trees and bushes. Shorty and I were driving around with a local real estate broker when we came upon a huge barred, chained, and padlocked set of doors that enclosed the pathway into a ten-acre, privately owned waterfront locale. We broke in through a side fence, and walked right into the almost exact setting for the over and underwater exploration in our shooting script.

I was on the phone within half an hour and found the owners of the property in Omaha, who after three phone calls gave me an authorization to use the grounds without cost for three weeks. I only needed it for two, but I figured the extra week would be in case of weather problems.

Everyone breathed much easier when our location was cleared. Within three working days we were set up for our first shot. We photographed all of the exteriors there, and came back with everything we needed within fourteen working days.

THE BLOB continued to do extremely well around the world. 4D MAN was just starting its distribution in international territories with Warner Brothers. It was now early 1960, when the indoor and some outdoor studio shooting for DINOSAURUS continued. We were on a schedule, which went fairly smooth, and we wrapped the shooting on time and under budget.

However, one thing was gnawing at me. For the first time since THE BLOB, I had no next project.

During this time, it was my habit to go get haircuts and manicures at the Beverly Hills Hotel Barber Shop. One day in the midst of my barbering, Johnny Carson sat down in the next barber chair to mine. He just had a trim, so I had the opportunity to chat with him. I told him about Ed McMahon doing a "bit" for me in DAUGHTER OF HORROR, a movie I acquired for distribution. Ed in a mask became a spooky character narrating a "midnight in the cemetery" scene.

Johnny roared and said, "I'll get him with this one."

A few days later, he roasted Ed on the show about the part.

Months went by and many celebrities inhabited the next chair without incident. One day, I looked over to see Fred Astaire, occupying the chair next to mine. I struck up a conversation with him about the Fred Astaire Dance Studios and my role in promoting the one in Philadelphia years earlier. He sat up after his barber removed his apron to reveal his trousers with a tie "not a belt" at his waist. I had always thought of this as a movie prop, but here it was in his daily life. Responses to my story about the dance studios led me to believe that he had merely loaned his name to the enterprise that took little of his time.

Fred was charming, personable and courteous. He has always been a screen favorite of mine and I was thrilled to meet him.

During the production of THE BLOB, I had an idea to do a Biblical story based upon the best named, but least known about book in the Bible, the Book of Jonah. When we had completed Post Production, I hired Ted Simonson to do the research for a script based upon Jonah and the Whale. I had a three-page bibliography and a thirty-page synopsis to show for it. I arranged to meet with Cecil B. DeMille, who had consulted on JAMBOREE, to see if he would be interested in working with me on such a production.

He said, "Jack, you've got a multi-million dollar title. I can't take anything away from your original thought. Go out and make the movie. I know it will be a box office smash."

Great advice, but not good enough for the producer of THE BLOB to go out and raise the multi-millions for such an enterprise. I filed it away for later use.

During the post production phase of DINOSUAURUS, I met Marion Hargrove, and told him about my idea of doing a modern day "Rip Van Winkle in the 21st Century" story. This would be the story of a man who fell asleep for fifty years and woke up in the 21st century with all of the gidgets and gadgets of the future to include human relationships and moral codes. The resultant screenplay was excellent. Sadly, I took a series of meetings at the various studios and wound up without a home for the project.

DINOSAURUS was substantially completed, and I proudly took the answer print to New York for screening by the Universal Studios brass. Their reaction was one of total amazement at the amount of humor in the piece, which they felt might be a detriment. They were pleased with the prehistoric creature special effects content, and felt it lived up to its name and its surrounding publicity.

There was a scheduled premiere in New Orleans within thirty-days of their screening, so some of the promotion was already in effect. I made an appearance at the New Orleans premiere and was gratified with a wonderful opening. I visited two more openings, which were also successful, then got back to my Hollywood office. I was still plagued with concern that no new projects were in the oven.

⌘

Chapter 11: Nudie Cutie

I was contacted by Richard Clair, a high school substitute English teacher, who was a roaring fan of THE BLOB. He presented me with a treatment he had written for a sequel titled, A CHIP OFF THE ‘OL BLOB. I dismissed it as a cute joke piece, until Richard let me read some of his other stuff. I thought he had a lot of talent.

Months later, Richard invited me to see his performance with his comedy partner, Jenna McMann, at the Ice House in Pasadena. The audience and I responded with plenty of laughter at their half-hour routine. Later, Richard and Jenna were visited by Carol Burnett and her husband. They were enthralled with Richard Clair, who went on to create the “Mamma” skit. The skit turned out to have a successful run on Carol’s series *The Carol Burnett Show,* followed by spin-off success with a four-year run on CBS as its own regular series, *Mama’s Family.* Still, there was no new movie idea.

Ward Ramsey, star of DINOSAURUS, called me for a lunch meeting to discuss how the picture was going and how his career wasn't. He had a seven-year deal with Universal. After the end of the first year, Ed Mull had decided to only renew his option for six more months. Ward was very distressed. I got on the phone and called a few of my friends at Universal. I arranged for him to get some parts in forthcoming pictures. They were short appearances, but at least he would get some more titles on his resume. He was grateful, and it was my great pleasure to help a very nice guy.

Still, I had no new project. I busied myself with the distribution consulting on my three existing films. A few more months went by and Ward Ramsey came to my office unannounced. He blurted out that the pictures I had helped him with were all small parts, and hardly a chance for him to be noticed.

I said, "Well, you had the lead in DINOSAURUS."

He told me, "Ed Mull, head of Universal wouldn't even look at the picture." His option was up again and he had an offer to do some television, which I urged him to accept.

He later came to my office again to announce that he was rejected by the casting people for the potential television employment, and he needed money real bad.

I asked, "What do you need?"

He said, "Two thousand bucks."

I told him, "You've got it."

He said, "I have no way to pay you back. Though, I do own an option to be involved in a nudie-cutie movie about a mathematics professor who invents a pair of glasses, through which he can see fully-clothed people nude."

I laughed and said, "That's not my bag, but I'll sure look at the script." The script was splendid. I met with the author and director, Haile Chace, who was the publicity director for Benz Motors in Southern California. This was a job he had taken because he ran out of jobs doing industrials and commercials. He got the idea for the movie and took whatever funds he had, including Ward Ramsey's money, and went to Europe where he shot a chase through Europe featuring Russians trying to steal the Professor's invention. I looked at the unedited footage and was fascinated. Taking over Ward Ramsey's position, I adopted the production reigns of the movie and quickly put together the financing to turn it into something special. I called it PARADISIO.

Still to be shot were a number of key scenes, plus all of the nude reverses of what the professor sees as he looks through his special lenses. After a few story sessions, I wondered, "As long as the nudity has not been photographed yet, and as long as the basic movie is in black and white, what if we shoot all of the reverses in color and 3D?"

Now, I had my next project.

I sent for Tim Barr so he could be production supervisor on all of the 3D shots. He led me to a double lens 3D camera that Howard Hughes created for several 3D movies that had been made years before. We were prepared to shoot in the anaglyph process, which used red and green glasses to be seen with depth perception. Since our average shot was less than two-minutes of screen time, this was a perfect option.

I contacted Hugh Hefner and he invited me to his then Chicago Playboy Mansion to talk about my production plans, part of which would include his key centerfold photographers to be given exclusive access to our nudie reverse scenes. He loaned me photographer Sam Wu, and we were off matching the hills of Beverly to the hills of Oxford, England, and the canals in Venice, CA for the roadside of the Baton Mouche boats in Paris, and other Los Angeles locations substituting for Geneva and Berlin.

Richard Clair made a rare screen appearance (he was an actor before he took up comedy) as a very 'smoky' Edward R. Murrow type moderator in the interview scene with Arthur Howard (Leslie Howard's brother), who played the professor in PARADISIO. This caused Richard and me to spend many hours together, during which time the chain smoker was not allowed to smoke in my allergic presence. At the end of production, he locked himself up in his apartment, refused all visitors, and quit smoking cold turkey. This was to the relief and astonishment of his mother, who would bring him food outside his apartment door every day. He really quit for good. But, it took three agonizing weeks on his part.

I got the biggest kick out of doing this picture. The creative problems and the superior result gave me a truly new outlook on filmmaking. Even the nudity was handled (you should pardon the expression) in good taste. I got Universal to allow me to have a private showing in their main studio theatre, to which my guest of honor was Hugh Hefner. Right after this showing we had a private party at my villa. During cocktail conversation, Hefner laid out his plans to create a new venue called Playboy Clubs, in which clients would have keys to enter the premises, to be entertained by female escorts called "Bunnies." I expressed my thorough approval of the idea and brought the subject of conversation back to the screening we had just held. Hefner said he was thrilled and would be personally producing and editing the expected article with photographs on my new movie PARADISIO. I had my national exposure assured in the June 1960 edition of the then super-potent Playboy Magazine.

I arranged to have a world premiere of PARADISIO take place at the Monica Theatre in West Hollywood. The owner was Frank Seltzer, a dear friend of mine from Philadelphia. Frank loved the picture and was a tremendous help in the promotion of their showing. We ran ads in the classified sections of the newspapers with a telephone number saying, "Lonesome gal needs a pal".

When people called the number, it was a recording made by sexy voiced, Pamela Curran, delivering a message about how she wanted to have company on her trip to PARADISIO. The word went out pretty fast, and we had four telephones going almost around the clock. The opening coincided with the newsstand date of The Playboy issue. Within seven weeks of a three month run, our share of the box office paid for all costs of making the picture, promoting it, and left us with about a $30,000 surplus. PARADISIO played for fifteen months solid on 42nd Street in

New York, jumping from one screen to the other and then back again. To my delight, I was getting phone calls from the heads of all the circuits offering playdates for my picture. It was a condition that lasted for about two-and-a-half years, and the financial results were astounding.

My son was then a buddy of Vicki Berle, Milton's daughter. It got back to me that after Milton saw some of the publicity on the picture he had said, "It should be called PAIR O' TITSIO."

My friend, Wolf Cohen, at Warner Brothers offered to release PARADISIO in the Far East under their system, provided I would take a trip to Japan, Hong Kong, Bangkok and Manila to promote the openings. PARADISIO was the most successful of the four pictures I had done to date under my banner. In fact, it grossed more than the other three combined. My company owned the picture, the copyright and the distribution. I was now in the millions.

⌘

Chapter 12: The Hollywood Bad Boys

In 1963, I was invited to the L.A. premiere of MACK THE KNIFE starring Lotte Lenya, who was giving an invitation only performance at the El Capitan Theatre on Hollywood Blvd. There, sitting right in front of my wife and me, were Steve McQueen and Neile Adams. We exchanged a few pleasantries before the show started. After "Mack the Knife" was sung a few times, Steve leaned around over to me and stated, "I don't want to hear it again." He and Neile then slipped out of the theatre. Although it was an excellent performance, Steve and Neile made their hasty exit before the final curtain.

Months later, I stopped into Hughes Market in Beverly Hills to pick up a few things. While checking out, there was Steve McQueen right in front of me. The cashier gushed, "Oh Mr. McQueen, I'm such a fan of yours. I loved you in NEVER LOVE A STRANGER. Which one of your movies was your favorite?"

Steve replied, "SOLDIER IN THE RAIN." That was a passable movie in which he costarred with Jackie Gleason.

I tapped him on the shoulder, and he acknowledged me immediately. I said, "Steve, why don't you tell her about THE BLOB? That's a really outstanding movie." As he left the market, he sarcastically answered back, 'It ain't Othello'."

Back in Hollywood, I had a good chance to assess the condition of my business, which was running wonderfully. As a result, there was no barrier against my acquiring a beach house for weekend getaways. The place we selected was the Malibu Colony, a private beach boasting 100 homes on ocean-front sand lots, some as narrow as thirty-one-feet each, although some were on wider lots.

A house became available, which the realtor said had a slight deterrent factor. It was next door to the Larry Hagman family, and was subject to the craziness that reportedly went on there.

Meeting and getting to know Larry Hagman and his wonderful wife, Maj, and their two adorable children, Heidi and Preston, and learning that Larry was the son of one of my favorites, Mary Martin, was indeed, a most fortunate plus to me.

Our one story beach house was 3000 square feet of living space in the main house, with an attached guesthouse that had two bedrooms and a bath adjoining a two-car garage. We made some architectural changes, naturally, improving closet space, modernizing kitchen and bathrooms, and generally refurbishing the entire structure. It was very livable and comfortable. My son was now ensconced in his West Hollywood apartment, and my daughter was in her Beverlywood House with her two little boys.

When I first started going on the beach, I would get up early, have a light breakfast, and take a swim in the very cool Pacific Ocean. It brought me back to my boyhood adventures in the Atlantic City Ocean. That was also cold, and I thought that's the way it had to be if you want to take a swim in the ocean.

About the third day, I was coming out of the ocean and picked up a towel on the steps to my deck. I was just standing there with a towel around me admiring the gorgeous waves, sun, and the seagulls when someone came up behind me and said, "I'm going to be just like you when I grow up."

It was Lee Marvin, who was one of my neighbors. I told him, "Lots of luck." We both laughed. I walked in the house telling Muriel how Lee Marvin had complimented me. She said, "He's older than you are don't you get it?"

I asked, "What is there to get?"

"Take a look at the ocean. Outside of a couple of surfers in wet suits, how many people do you see swimming?" she replied.

It dawned on me that the Pacific Ocean is a pretty damned cold place. I determined to reserve my swimming in it for warmer currents, but it did make a walker out of me. There was scarcely a day that I walked less than five miles at the tide line on the sand. Every day, Larry Hagman would say to me, "It's just another shitty day in Paradise."

Larry Hagman's better half, Maj, (former SAS airline stewardess) was a handsome formidable woman. She was a master chef, perfect housewife and mother, but also a self-trained architect. She designed all of the extensions and redecorating improvements to their next-door house. One of her primo products was the famous Maj Hagman Jacuzzi hot tub that extended from their beachfront entrance. She went on to design many more spas for various famous clients.

I had the good fortune to spend many an hour in Maj's hot tub where I encountered Peter Fonda, Carol Linley, Millie Perkins, Godfrey Cambridge, and many others at various times. We were all in the buff, but for therapeutic not sexual reasons.

One day I was lolling in the tub solo, when the surrounding curtain opened and Natalie Wood stood at the entrance, holding her eighteen-month old daughter who was her spitting image. She asked if they could join me. Being the gentleman that I am, I made them welcome. Her child was fathered by Richard Gregson, during a marriage when she divorced Robert Wagner. We spent an unforgettable half hour schmoozing until I had to reluctantly leave for an appointment.

About two years later, I was walking on the Malibu Colony Road with Barbra Streisand helping her look at an available beach house, when Natalie Wood and Robert Wagner suddenly appeared, walking toward us. They had rekindled their romance. The four of us walked together discussing what soon became the remarriage of Natalie and Robert. Natalie's life tragically ended two years later in a mysterious drowning, as she fell from a boat off the coast of Catalina.

Although four pictures were now under my belt, I had expanded my organization and my overhead to the point where my cash flow was rather flat. I was invited to Las Vegas to see a show at the Sands Hotel that turned out to be a musical interpretation of Mother Goose stories and nursery rhymes with a naughty twist. I couldn't see filming this show to have a theatrical purpose, but I worked on the idea with Richard Clair. We cobbled together a story wherein the protagonist was plagued by a childhood problem. In the midst of love-making, he would fail to get it up upon hearing any reference to Mother Goose stories and nursery rhymes. This was a cute idea in 1969, but not for major studio distribution. I intended to make the picture and add it to my release schedule with my distribution company. I succeeded in financing the project with a cash investment from a telemarketing company, in return for a 40% interest in the picture. I proceeded with cast selection consisting of Tommy Kirk, who had just been fired by Disney amidst accusation and scandal, Ann Helm, co-star in a number of forgettable teen movies, Jacques Bergerac, famed ex-husband of Ginger Rogers, and for insurance, guest appearances by Henny Youngman and Joe Pine.

We pulled every favor we could get together. We promoted the women's costumes from famed designer, Gus Tassel, and the men's outfits from Botany 500. Gratis locations used were Ciro's Nightclub, now the Laugh Factory, and other '60s watering holes. Mercedes and General Motors furnished the cars and the film and processing was completely on a pay-later basis.

When I told the investor his payment was due, he cried "poverty." Since I had everything lined up, I decided to use whatever immediate funds were at my disposal and since I couldn't afford any director, I decided to direct the picture myself. My wife Muriel and her partner, Jim Bechtold, designed and dressed the sets with completely borrowed set pieces. I assembled a skeleton crew of six people and let everyone know that it wasn't a question of how many days of shooting. It was a question of how many hours of shooting we could afford.

We completed the picture in ten days at a very modest cost. This was followed by spending sixty intense days on editing and Post Production. It looked like a million dollar movie. Between the sexy humor and the decent performances, MOTHER GOOSE A-GO GO was an entertaining picture.

The title proved hard to pronounce and more difficult to put on a marquee. A Chicago exhibitor who screened the picture called and suggested, "You should call the picture THE UNSCREWED BRIDE."

I cleaned up the title to be, THE UNKISSED BRIDE, which enjoyed a passable companion feature gross theatrically, eventually becoming a semi-strong VHS title.

After big studio releases and a major PARADISIO coup, it was a bit of a letdown to have a program picture that was not a big winner added to the list. At least I was back in distribution with a new title.

One day, I was standing in the private, gated driveway for the homes in the stretch of Malibu Colony Beach. Some guy, driving a non-descript car leaned out of the window and asked, "Where can I find Freddie Fields? (Famous 1960s Talent Agent and Producer)" The guy was Steve McQueen.

I said, "How soon we forget."

He said, "Jack! What the hell are you doin' here?"

I pointed to my house and said, "This is my house. If you want Freddie Fields, he's up the road. I showed him the exact house."

We shook hands and he went to find Freddie Fields.

A couple of weeks later, I arrived home from one of my beach walks and was met at the door by my wife, Muriel, who informed me, "Steve McQueen's been here looking for you."

I asked, "What does he want?"

"He wants to rent this house for a year. I told him he'd have to talk to you. He should be showing up any minute."

I went out on my deck and heard somebody yelling, "Hey Jack. Hey, Jack." I looked down on the sand and there was Steve McQueen in shorts standing with Freddie Fields, who was apparently his manager at that point in time.

I walked out on the sand and shook hands with them both. I asked, "Steve, what's on your mind?"

He said, "I'm going to rent your house for a year."

I said, "Steve, you don't have enough money to get me out of this house for a year."

Steve said, "That's silly. I'll do a picture for you for free."

Freddie Fields stood there with his mouth gaping.

I inquired, "Steve, do you know what you just said?"

He replied, "Oh, I meant a walk on – and I'll pay you a lot."

So Freddie joined in, "I didn't know you guys knew each other."

I said, "We're old acquaintances."

Steve added, "I've known Jack quite a while."

I said, "Steve, did you ever tell Freddie about THE BLOB?"

Freddie Fields in his most austere, celebrity-management tone said, "What's THE BLOB?"

Steve jumped in with "Freddie, I was on the balls of my ass…"
I finished the sentence with, "and THE BLOB turned him into a big time star."

They were both silent. I said, "Freddie it's always nice to see you. Steve, it's a pleasure to see you. This house is my castle and is not for sale or rent. I'm sure Freddie could guide you to a good real estate broker who can find you a rental in this neighborhood." I shook hands with both of them. They didn't say a word. I walked up the sand and on to my deck without turning around. When I got on to the deck, I turned and took a quick look at them. They were both standing there watching me silently as I went into the house.

Steve ended up not renting a house in the Colony that year. Sadly, that was the last time I saw Steve.

In rapid order, my distribution company acquired the rights to a horror comedy which we titled, MY SON THE VAMPIRE, featuring Bella Lugosi and the Carry On Gang (famous for a series of goofy, English comedies). The story centered on Dracula's nephew who couldn't stand the sight of blood, so he plotted to take over the world with an army of 50,000 robots. The one problem was that he could only afford to make one. I got Alan Sherman to write and perform the title song, and we did get a smattering of art house play to no great box office results. The picture became profitable due to a deal I made with Screen Gems for television use, and subsequent deals on the DVD distribution market.

Two Westerns made early in the career of Jack Nicholson, THE SHOOTING (also starring Millie Perkins) and RIDE IN THE WHIRLWIND, were sitting around in dispute that clouded the rights. I went to the attorney in charge and made a deal to distribute them theatrically. Jack Nicholson joined me in a promo tour starting in Dallas, Texas. His presence lent luster to the premiere, but the audience reaction to the pictures was lacking. Throughout our interactions, Jack was a humorous guy. He bragged to me about how he had made the two movies on "credit cards."

I was shaken, but didn't comment.

He was always a jovial, dedicated filmmaker. He confided to me that he knew he wasn't poor because he had accumulated $40,000 in the bank. Our tour in Dallas happened to end with a press meeting at the McLendon Theatres office at the Dallas airport, at the end of which he said, "I guess that does it."

I said, "Jack, I thank you very much."

He said, "I'm off for a left bank hotel in Paris, and I wish you success." Then as he donned his British sports cap he said, "So long, Jack," grabbed his bag and ran for the plane. Sometimes meeting celebrities feels like finally having a friendly conversation with the cheerleader in high school you were too afraid to ask to the prom. You realize, with beautiful women and celebrities alike, they're all just people. At least most of them… sometimes, the moments feel surprisingly quiet and human. In my experience, Jack's a wonderful, funny, very decent human being, not the character his legend might have led us to expect.

Regrettably, I never formally distributed either film, both produced by Roger Corman and directed by Monte Hellman. I acquired the rights, and spent six months working on a campaign that wasn't to the taste of the copyright holders. We decided I would give them back the rights, and we parted ways. The business model Corman was using was such that even if a couple of his films didn't take, they were all made cheaply enough that he was fine. Due to a changeover in Universal brass, Monte Hellman's seminal film TWO-LANE BLACKTOP was buried upon its initial release, and he never had the career he should have had or the success he deserved.

We all know what happened to Jack Nicholson. Both of these so-called "acid westerns" were never released in America. Though Hellman and the films themselves were vindicated by cult following and revival screenings they would receive over the years. Quentin Tarantino wrote a famous article calling RIDE IN THE WHIRLWIND the greatest Western ever made. Jack Nicholson received sole screenwriting credit for the film, as it's a little-known fact that he wrote a handful of subversive films before his career as an actor took off. Criterion recently rereleased both titles together in what is supposed to be the definitive home video presentation.

In contrast to Nicholson, some of the celebrities I've encountered in various capacities live up to their persona in every way you would expect of them. As a perfect case-in-point, the famed Rat Pack members – Frank Sinatra, Dean Martin, Sammy Davis, Jr., and Joey Bishop – made a few Las Vegas casino hotels pretty rich while interrupting each other's starring shows with unannounced appearances. It was thrilling to go and see one of them perform and hope that there would be an unannounced interruption as the others joined the show. This went on for a while, until one day Dean hurt Frank's feelings, and they stopped talking to each other.

Almost six months into the feud, I was invited to an ACLU event headed by Frank Sinatra with Burt Lancaster. It was at Dean Martin's house donated by his wife Jeannie.

At 8:00 PM on the appointed day, Frank was doing his table-to-table singing routine. When he stopped for a break, Jeannie stepped up to the mic and announced to the ninety-person, star-studded audience, that Dean was finishing his last Sands Las Vegas show and would arrive at the

Frank Sinatra, Burt Lancaster, Anthony (3rd from left) and me (Far left) at the party with other Hollywood luminaries, 1965.

party by 10:30 PM. You could hear whispers, "What will happen when they meet?" Speculation was rampant, but Burt made his ACLU speech and Frank started speaking, with no comment about Dean.

I wandered over to a table for two, near the entrance to avoid the gossip, when a very drunken, tuxedo clad, still in makeup Dean Martin, silently joined me. Nobody noticed Dean's arrival. He was incoherent when I tried to converse with him. I said, "Frank Sinatra is here." He sat up, blinked and yelled, "Where?"

I pointed across the room to Frank, and Dean yelled, "Sonova bitch," and passed out. Frank, Burt, and others rushed over and lifted Dean up, who looked at Frank and whined, "I'm sorry," before passing out again. Frank and Burt supported the polluted Dean toward his bedroom while Frank smiled, "Good night, Drunkie," as he kissed Dean on the head. The feud was over.

⌘

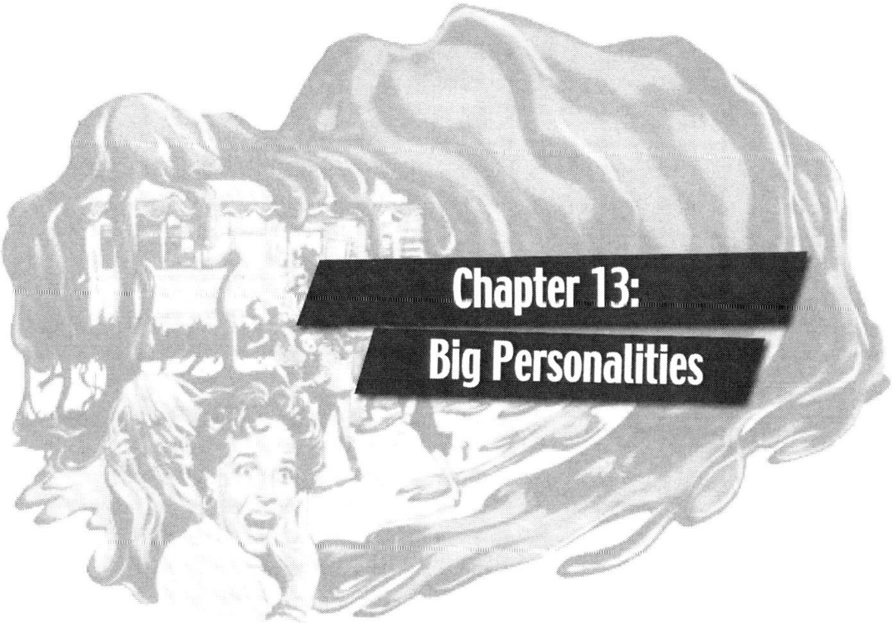

Chapter 13: Big Personalities

In 1971, Muriel and I were weekend guests of Bullets Durgom, manager of many famous stars, and his wife, Marion, at their Palm Springs home. It was New Year's Eve. At about 8:00 PM, Bullets ordered us into his car for a surprise celebration. We drove at least half an hour and arrived at a secluded estate in Palm Desert. About ten cars were in the parking area. A uniformed attendant approached us asking for identification. We were admitted to "Paco's Place," the home of Frank Sinatra.

There were about twenty guests, among whom were Frank's latest squeeze, Barbara Marx, and her ex-husband, Zeppo. Spiro Agnew, then Vice President of the United States with his wife, and a staff of four were there. Agnew was soloing on the piano of a six-piece orchestra, as Frank Sinatra stood making faces at the assemblage. Bullets introduced us to him. After a few minutes of small talk, Frank said, "I'd like to show my humble abode to the producer of one of my favorite movies, THE BLOB. Follow me." Spiro Agnew joined the five of us for a tour of the fabulous house. On the kitchen butcher-block table was the largest roast turkey I'd ever seen. I asked Frank where he got it. "I caught it under the sink," he said, "so I shot it."

The food, booze, and banter were most memorable and soon Auld Lang Syne started playing. Everyone toasted the New Year. A little past 1:00 AM, I persuaded Bullets to leave for home, and Frank saw us to the door. A very drunk Bullets kept fumbling a thank-you. Frank cut him short with, "You and the Harris's are welcome guests. I enjoyed you bringing them. Now get them back home safely."

Bullets tried again. Frank shut him up with, "Here's a prize, now get out!" He gave a speechless Bullets one of his Emmys. Bullets grabbed it and headed for the car.

We were soon speedily on our way, being driven by an erratic Bullets Durgom. Suddenly, we heard sirens and two uniformed motorcyclists pulled us over. I thought they wanted us for speeding. The police, after identifying Bullets and getting him to exit the car, asked for the Emmy. Bullets claimed no knowledge of an Emmy. The three of us sat quietly observing the proceedings. After looking through the car, the cops wisely had Marion take the wheel and forced Bullets into the rear seat. We headed silently home.

New Year's Day, Marion served breakfast at about 10:00 AM. An extra guest showed up, Lennie Hayton, husband of the then-touring Lena Horne. Lennie pointed at the fireplace mantle and asked, "Bullets, when did you get an Emmy?" Bullets calmly replied, "It was just an honorary one." The rest of us quietly looked at the reappeared statuette.

After Lennie left, I asked Bullets how he found it. "I had it tucked away in my overcoat cargo pocket all the time."

I noted, "Frank is looking for it."

"Nonsense," he bragged. "He gave it to me as a gift and I'm keeping it."

Marion said, "Bullets, Jack's right. Give it back."

"Frank has four others," Bullets replied, "He wanted me to keep this one." The telephone rang. It was Frank Sinatra's secretary. She demanded the return of the Emmy, explaining that Mr. Sinatra was playing a prank. Thirty minutes later, the doorbell announced the arrival of the Sinatra Property Manager who came to retrieve the Emmy. Bullets tearfully gave it to the manager. We then all quietly watched football on TV.

Back home, there was a steady stream of complaints about brake wear and tear on the steep road leading to our Trousdale house. We moved from hillside Trousdale Estates to Palm Drive in Beverly Hills.

One morning, while returning home from my constitutional, I was approaching my house when I noticed this comely, apron wearing, and duster-capped lady on a ladder, brushing debris from her roof.

She saw me and said, "Good Morning," as the huge dust broom slipped from her grasp.

I yelled, "Stand still," and ran to retrieve her broom. I handed her the broom and recognized Jean Peters, famous actress and ex-wife of Howard Hughes.

She introduced me to Happy, her pet Burmese cat, whom I petted as we chatted. Neither of us mentioned Howard Hughes as she welcomed me to the neighborhood. When she found out my Hollywood connection, she told me she was about to marry Stanley Hough, a producer at 20th Century Fox. Later, I met Stanley, standing in the driveway and he seemed like a very nice chap. They were our next-door neighbors.

Happy started hanging out at my house. Each morning he would join me on my walks through the park along Santa Monica Blvd. We had a habit of interrupting our walk to sit on a nearby park bench about a mile from our houses to the amusement of passing motorists. We would end our trip by walking back to Palm Drive where I'd drop him off at his house. Happy was the closest thing to a dog I'd ever seen. When he got lonesome, he'd wait by our back patio until I went out to sit with him or invite him in. Happy and I were happy pals.

One day, I was amazed to find a large communications truck parked across the street. Four workmen were loading miles of wire and switchboard apparatus from the upscale house, which was as elegant as the surrounding ones. Certainly not appearing to be the kind of place indicated by the communication equipment. I then noticed six men, all in hats, supervising the loading process. The six men and all of the movers and equipment soon vacated the house. I discovered it housed one of Howard Hughes communication centers and a couple of agents responsible for Jean Peter's well being. The move was triggered by her former marriage to Howard Hughes who felt she would now be properly protected.

Jean, after a successful life and marriage, passed away two days before her 74th birthday in 2000.

One day, Lynda, called me for a private meeting. I found this very strange because we already saw each other at least once a week. She came to my office looking very drawn and I awaited the reason for her visit.

"Dad, I need your advice," Lynda blurted.

I said, "OK, what's the question?"

She said, "Is it all right for me to let somebody use my copying machine to record top secret United States Government documents?"

I was immediately thrown back into my days at the Pentagon wherein I helped write a law preventing such actions, and I told her that.

She asked, "What would happen if I did such a thing?"

I said, "Well, I would defend you with everything I had."

She asked another question, "If I didn't do the copying would I be guilty of breaking the law?"

I said, "Well, that puts you one step away from the crime. My advice is, don't do it."

She started to cry. I put my arm around her and dabbed her eyes with a tissue and asked, "What's the matter, honey,"

She looked at me with tears streaming down her face and said, "I've already done it."

I was overwhelmed and asked, "What's the good of my advice at this point?"

She said, "Well, I should have asked you first. It all happened so quickly that I had to give a snap answer. Apparently, it was the wrong one."

"Who did you allow to do this on your copier?" I asked.

She said, "You know Tony Russo, the guy I've been seeing."

I said, "He seems harmless and honest enough."

She replied, "His partner is Daniel Ellsberg."

I remembered stories wherein Ellsberg released Top Secret documents to the *New York Times.* This wound up in a front page story concerning his potential guilt under the law, becoming known as "The Pentagon Papers" scandal. I told her to distance herself from the act, and to let me know what protective measures I could inaugurate to help.

I immediately got a call from Rona Barrett, the then reigning news hen. She told me that she had to feature the Ellsberg story in her column and on her television show. She wanted me to know that she would do her best to protect my identity as the father of the culprit, Lynda. I told her she could use my name if necessary.

I headed to Europe for some openings of 4D MAN, and while on the plane from London to Paris, I noticed a newspaper story about a new film featuring Raquel Welch as one of the stars. She had become known worldwide through the medium of magazine covers. She probably holds a record for being on thirty magazine covers in a two-month period internationally.

When I got to Paris, I contacted Henry Deutchmeister, my old opponent on the acquisition of the Laurel and Hardy feature. He arranged for me to have a screening of the picture, THE OLDEST PROFESSION, and I was quite taken with the possibilities. He warned me in advance of the screening that I wasn't going to steal his picture like I did the other one. He appointed a New York attorney of French descent to represent him in the negotiation.

It was very curious how a guy in his eighties undertook to make a movie about hookers from the Stone Age through the Space Age, enticing an internationally known director and star for each of these segments. Raquel Welch starred in the segment called, "Le Grande Epoch," and was fabulous in it.

My son Anthony wrote a title song which was good enough to be released via Capitol Records. Raquel Welch helped to promote it through some of her inimitable public appearances.

Here was a brand new film, produced like a major Hollywood picture, featuring Raquel Welch and some of the hottest female stars in the world.

Though I had my work cut out for me, I landed the U.S. and English speaking Canada rights. It was a big disappointment as a theatrical entry. However through the years, between theatres, television, and home video, it has never lost its popularity and has treated me very well.

I was entering my Paris hotel when I bumped into a dear exhibitor friend from Hollywood, Lou Sher, who after a brief greeting inquired, "Have you seen this week's TIME Magazine?"

I said, "Not yet."

He said, "Well here it is." He handed me the magazine folded over to one of its pages. The entire page was a photograph of my daughter, Lynda, along with the story of the "Pentagon Papers" caper. My mouth hung open and before I could say a word, Lou said to me, "Lynda sure takes a nice picture." This was an early comment, but far from the only one that I would field on the matter. Lynda was later cleared of all charges by the FBI. I changed the subject and told Lou about my excitement for acquiring the rights to THE OLDEST PROFESSION.

Having successfully launched THE OLDEST PROFESSION, and having put the matters surrounding the Pentagon Papers behind me, I was able to return home to Beverly Hills in hopes of trying to catch my breath for a bit. A prominent surgeon, Dr. Irving Lichtenstein, and his charming wife, Billy, both former Philadelphians now living in Beverly Hills, became close, personal friends. Their four daughters, age six, ten, twelve and fourteen were a lot of fun. Irving's chief hobby was sailing his twenty-foot boat. Muriel and I enjoyed many sailing trips with the dedicated doctor, in spite of his occasional bouts of seasickness. He taught me how to handle the tiller in case he had one of his spells.

We were once invited on a special cruise, to which he had also invited his patient, Burt Lancaster, and his at the time girlfriend. Burt proved affable and jovial. He took sailing very seriously, giving Irving a constant tutorial on the means, mode, and methods of controlling a motor sailor. Irving was bugged by Burt's constant tirades, but the rest of us had a ball. We were well on our way to Catalina when Burt suddenly made his way to the bow and whipped out a telescope and directed Irving to change course. I had my binoculars and saw what had captured Burt's attention. We came upon a thirty-foot motor sailor that was slowly put-putting in a circle. We heard a baby crying and when the boat came around there was a crying young mother holding her screaming baby on the deck. Floundering about in the water was a guy who apparently fell overboard and who was unsuccessfully trying to reboard.

Burt, in his element, threw a line with a life preserver to the swimmer, and it took three of us to haul him onto our deck. He was dripping, fully clothed and showering us and the deck with seawater. Besides being waterlogged, he was saturated with alcohol. He promptly curled up and passed out in a sunny spot while Burt radioed the Coast Guard. We shouted calming advice to the crying couple on the boat. The Coast Guard arrived and boarded the errant vessel, shut off the engine and calmed down the crying pair.

Suddenly, the drunken "guest" awoke and jumped up almost knocking over Burt and his telescope as he dove into the water, swimming into the arms of the Coast Guard. Strangely, nobody recognized our hero.

At dinner that night, Burt leaned over to me and said, "I always knew attending navigation school would pay off someday."

⌘

Chapter 14: Two Hits and a Miss

Jean Ronald Getty (Ron), briefly head of Getty Oil Company in Germany, was suddenly excluded by his father from the business and the family trust. This was because J. Paul Getty resented the cost of the divorce from J. Ronald's mother.

Ron headed to Los Angeles, created Getty Film Laboratories and in 1971, funded SOMETHING MORE. It was a miscegenation movie production boasting a Quincy Jones score. Executive Producer, Leon Fromkess, seeking distribution for the movie, invited me to a screening. I liked what I saw and agreed to distribute the picture, provided I could change the title.

After some research, I titled this love story between a beautiful black girl and a sandy-haired white guy, HONKY. The distribution concentrated on the black communities nationally and racked up a substantial gross. This model, innovative at the time, was followed by the "Blaxploitation" films of the 1970s, and in the ensuing decades became extremely lucrative for producers such as Tyler Perry. After ten months when the theatre showings for HONKY slowed down, Ron took back the movie and looked for ancillary distribution options.

Not too much later he and his company went bankrupt and he went back to Germany, where he was being supported by members of the Getty family.

In 1972, I was offered a movie that had not been picked up for distribution called BONE. It dealt with a white Beverly Hills couple terrorized by a black intruder who has an affair with the wife. The writer/director was Larry Cohen, a well-known TV writer, and this was his first theatrical feature film. The negotiation was arduous. Larry had expected to fascinate a major studio with his film. I doggedly stayed in the negotiation because I now knew something Larry didn't know about suitable movie releasing in urban neighborhoods.

We made a deal which included me putting up a sizeable advance. My first move to try and find a new title was made almost impossible. Larry Cohen adamantly defended his original title, BONE. Sometimes, people don't care if an idea is brilliant or terrible, as long as it's theirs. I set up a sneak preview at the now defunct Pico Theatre in L.A., figuring that the audience might help find a new title. One of the attendees was famed reviewer, Arthur Knight, who years before had interviewed me on his TV show heralding the release of THE BLOB. We remained friends throughout the years.

I asked Arthur his opinion. He told me it was far from a great movie. I started to defend the movie when Larry Cohen appeared and took me aside to ask me to respect Arthur's opinion and not argue with him. Arthur Knight proved to be correct.

At Larry's insistence we released BONE with great fanfare, and a campaign he created to general audiences both in New York and in Los Angeles, to less than satisfying results. BONE was successful for Larry, as he was able to parlay his theatrical playoff into further movie-making opportunities. He became a sought after screenwriter, writing and directing IT'S ALIVE, CELLULAR, and recently PHONE BOOTH.

If any young film students are reading this and want to ultimately direct films, there's an important lesson for you to learn from this. If anybody ever offers you a chance to make a movie, take it. Or, if you can make your movie, make it. Once you've made a movie, you're no longer looking for a job or trying to get a film financed as a "first time director." Even if your first film wasn't a banner success or the great redefinition of cinema, sometimes, just having competently made a film, and it being something of a success is enough.

Larry Cohen became my Malibu neighbor and we spent many pleasant times together. His then wife, Janelle, joined my walking group at 8:00 AM each day and was home in time for Larry's wake-up. His son, Bobby, was a backgammon genius. When there was a lull at my beach house, I'd take my board to the Cohen's for some stiff competition. The three young Cohen girls, Pam, Missy and Jill, were a cheerful rooting team at the backgammon sessions. Larry and I remain friends to this day. We both mourn the passing of Arthur Knight.

In 1973, Susan Stafford, then a fairly well known news-hen and her boyfriend, Robert McLendon, who owned a big circuit of theatres in Texas and several newspapers and radio and TV stations, gave a Mock Academy Awards show at the Ambassador Hotel in L.A. I always figured it was because Susan couldn't get into the Governor's Ball at the regular Academy, so her boyfriend threw the party.

There were tons of celebrities and I was sitting with a group of movie studio people. I had been pre-notified that I would be one of the award recipients of the evening.

A sumptuous dinner was served along with suitable libations and the show started. Apparently, the awards were given out in alphabetical order. Soon an assistant requested I join him backstage, where I saw several recipients standing in line waiting to be introduced. The guy in front of me looked familiar, and I soon recognized him as Clint Eastwood. I had just seen DIRTY HARRY. Instead of introducing myself with a kiss-up line, I said, "Clint, I saw the picture, and I thought it was wonderful. I can't help feeling hurt that my friend Frank Sinatra was aced out of the role."

He turned to me and asked, "Jack, remember the key scene in the movie?"

I said, "Sure, 'make my day.'"

He laughed, "That's right, but think about it. I was standing with a six-shooter in one hand, and a half eaten hot dog in the other. If Frank had played the part, he would have wanted to be eating a ritzy steak sandwich."

He was called to the podium and I wished him luck, and he said, "Same to you, Jack."

It turns out that Clint won Best Actor for DIRTY HARRY. I won for Best Producer for PARADISIO.

While attending a film festival in Rome, my next-door neighbor at the Excelsior Hotel was John Dunning. He headed up a Canadian distribution company, which ultimately became Lions Gate Films. When we finally got a chance to spend a few minutes together, John told me about this interesting movie that the Danes had put together called WITHOUT A STITCH ON.

On my way back to California I stopped in Montréal for the sole purpose of screening WITHOUT A STITCH ON. Wading through the snow on my way to a taxi, I was impressed with what I saw. My five hour flight back to Los Angeles seemed like twenty minutes. All I could think of was how to launch WITHOUT A STITCH in the United States, provided I was able to acquire the rights

Back in L.A., I investigated the situation and found that Allied Artists, headed by my old boss Steve Broidy, had been entertaining the acquiring of this picture themselves. I huddled with Jack Sattinger, my legal eagle, who was also Steve Broidy's son-in-law. Together, we hatched a plan to acquire the U.S. rights. It meant going around the rep Steve had been talking to in Paris, and frontally negotiating with Frank Doneston in Copenhagen, representing the Danish company that produced the film.

The story dealt with a Danish teenage girl, played by Ann Grete. She had found a steady beau, and while willing to make love with him, she was unfortunately frigid. Her mother took her to a sex therapist, who taught her how to play in every way. She takes her summer vacation from high school to travel around Europe, practicing what her therapist preached. She winds up back in the arms of her first love. Because the film was directed by Annalise Meineiche, who had previously directed the Academy Award-winning best foreign film, SEVENTEEN, our heroine looked just as sweet and innocent at movie's end as she did before she sought therapy.

My deal with the Danes was concluded in a one-day session during my trip to Copenhagen, but they asked me to stay an extra day. My business had been completed, and I was flattered by their request, until I found out they expected me to rewrite the English subtitles for the picture. I'll never forget that February day crossing the main square in front of Hans Christian Andersen's bronze statue with the cold wind blowing straight through my lined Burberry trench coat and two sweaters underneath. I don't do too well in the cold, but I stayed the extra day and worked until almost an hour before plane time to complete the translation rewrite. Sometimes, and especially in dealing with film sets, film distribution and promotion, you have to do whatever the job requires.

Back in L.A., though I nursed a serious respiratory ailment for almost a week, I knew I had done the right thing. All the contractual paperwork was completed within a week, and the picture negatives were shipped on a three-day system. Unfortunately, the U.S. Department of Justice interrupted the shipment and sent me a notice of a lawsuit in Federal Court naming me as the importer of sexually explicit entertainment.

I contacted Milton Friedman, the attorney who made his reputation defending against obscenity charges. His defense of the film centered on the picture not exceeding community standards for explicit films. The thirty-day trial climaxed (no pun intended) when the jury was taken to a small theatre in Hollywood for a special screening of their current explicit film, STEWARDESSES. The judge, Andrew Hauck, instructed the jury to find WITHOUT A STITCH obscene and un-importable to the United States. However, the jury ignored his instructions and unanimously voted the picture admissible and not in violation of community standards.

I secured a premiere showing at Loews flagship theatre on Broadway. The crowds gave the theatre probably their biggest gross ever at that time. During the first month of the showing I was inundated with offers from all over the United States. I was able to command 60% of the gross collections for at least the first two weeks of showing and 50% thereafter. It didn't take long for the multi-millions to add up, and the roaring media attention helped to reduce my advertising costs to a minimum. I was amazed at how rapidly the money came in and how many first class, first run theatres ran the picture.

In 1970, Millie Perkins and her writer husband, Bob Thom, invited us to an intimate home-cooked supper at their beach house. The guest of honor, a little late in arriving, was Jennifer Jones. When dinner was served, we casually sat around on the floor with our meals on convenient footstools, and Jennifer came over to share mine. She was much more beautiful that I'd ever seen her in any movie, plus charming and vulnerable. She hadn't yet met her third husband, Norton Simon.

Our small talk got around to movies, and I told her that in 1955 in Dallas, I had the pleasure of having lunch with her father who owned the biggest drive-in theatre there. She asked if he spoke kindly about her. I said, "He spoke of you in a proud, reverential manner and filled us in on the latest gossip concerning David [O. Selznick, her late second husband] and yourself." She was duly surprised and pleased. I went on to tell her that before my producing days I distributed the re-issue of DUEL IN THE SUN, one of the pictures she and O. Selznick had made.

She told me that her acting days had come to a close. She was happy enjoying the fruits of her labors and the honors she had received. Then she asked me, "Do you have any movies in contemplation?"

I said, "Well, I'm always thinking two shows ahead."

Jennifer asked, "Could you find a job for my son, Robert Walker, Jr.? If you could, I would consider it a personal favor."

I promised that I would keep him in mind.

Although I was, in fact, always working hard and thinking ahead, now that I had gained more financial stability with my latest wave of post-Blob success, it seemed fitting to begin scouting new challenges. My hobby was collecting frogs, not real ones, but those made of gold, silver, crystal and porcelain. Many years ago, I acquired a Ming jade frog of very good size. It is the crown jewel of my collection. Along with frogs, I was always interested in cars, and my additional hobby became collecting vintage Rolls Royces. At one time I had fourteen of them. They were fun to keep shined up and to take short rides in, but they were too good for the street. I eventually sold all of them. My favorite memory in any of them was when I was descending from my Trousdale home in a 1965 Rolls convertible to the stop sign when Elvis Presley leaned out of the window of his custom Dusenberg to exclaim, "Now that's a car!" That was quite an endorsement, and from The King himself! I next purchased a 1970 Mercedes 280 3.5 custom convertible, which was my regular car for business and social trips.

One day in 1970, I got a phone call from Dan Tabas, an old pal of mine back in Pennsylvania. Dan owned a steel mill and various real estate properties. His personal fun property was a glorified motel in Downingtown, Pennsylvania, near the diner that was used as a location during the shooting of THE BLOB. Dan had become friendly with Mickey Rooney, who had played golf at the course he owned and was adjacent to his property.

Mickey would run over to Pennsylvania from various summer theatres he appeared in, and Dan made him an invited guest of honor. This was mutually beneficial, because Mickey attracted a lot of traffic to the motel.

Dan finally got around to the reason he was calling me, which was to ask my opinion on whether he should finance a movie starring Mickey. I told him the most important thing to do before he would get involved in such an enterprise would be to have a foolproof screenplay. Dan knew what I was saying but didn't understand it at all. He confessed that he knew nothing about movies, screenplays, or anything involved in the making thereof. That's why he was calling me.

I said, "What can I do for you?"

He said, "Talk to Mickey, and then advise me."

I agreed.

The next day, coincidentally, I was in a Beverly Hills drug store when in walked Mickey Rooney. I introduced myself.

He noted, "You're the friend of Dan Tabas."

I said, "Yes."

He said, "Just the man I want to see. I was going to call you today."

He asked me to sit at the soda counter, which I did. He proceeded to perform the whole movie he intended to produce. He gestured, he danced, he cried, he smiled, and he kept narrating what was happening on the screen. I noticed both customers and store personnel stopped in their tracks and quietly watched the bravura performance by this great, famous actor.

When it was over, I congratulated Mickey and told him I'd certainly tell Dan about our chance meeting.

He added, "Make sure he brings the money." He didn't ask me what I thought. He didn't ask me if I was enthusiastic. He was so certain of his success that he gave me a hug and his gratitude for listening.

We both left the drug store going in different directions. I was truly touched by what I had seen and heard. The problem was, since the story was a heavyweight melodrama about a director going mad, I couldn't see Mickey in the part. Further, I couldn't see why such a film should ever be made because it had Rooney solely on screen for ninety-minutes talking to invisible people, while running the gamut of human and some inhuman emotions. I communicated my disappointment to Dan who thanked me profusely and promised never to forget my sincere appraisal.

I said, "I'm not selling, but if you ever want to do a picture with Mickey that has box office potential, let me know. I'll help you put it together."

Nine months went by and I was plenty busy with my production and distribution routine. The telephone rang, and Mickey Rooney was calling me.

He said, "Jack, I'm having a screening of my movie, THE MANIPULATOR, tonight at 7:00 PM at UCLA. I would like for you to come and see what you missed out on."

I had appointments, but I cancelled them and went to the screening. It was everything that I had imagined it would be. Mickey did that good a job in the drug store tryout. I knew it would never be released. I don't know where he got the money, but it was a pure exercise of professional ego. I stayed for the Question and Answer session from the student audience, and cringed at some of the barbs thrown at Rooney who accepted them with aplomb and shrugged them off. Director Yabo Yablonsky deserves most of the blame for this very miserable movie. The very limited audience felt they were manipulated.

Mickey Rooney went on to perform creditably on stage, in film and on TV. He's still the greatest.

Malibu beckoned, and I had a tough time answering the call, but the house was there and waiting. I would take as many days as possible to enjoy the relaxation it offered. My Father was there visiting from Philly, and he and Larry Hagman, my neighbor to the North, seemed to be getting along. One night we were sitting on the deck having one of Larry's many champagne drinks. Larry had a system of never talking on Sunday. Instead, he carried a pad and pencil with him as he did his beach exercises. In case anybody talked to him, he would answer in writing. He also was "on the wagon" each Sunday, restricting his alcoholic intake to champagne only. This seemed like a bit of a weak loophole, as he became notorious for the cases of bubbly he had delivered from the supermarket right across the road.

On this particular Sunday, Larry wrote me a message, "Uncle Jack, I've never seen THE BLOB."

My Father looked over my shoulder and said, "Jesus, your best buddy and he's never seen THE BLOB."

I said, "All right, all right, we'll fix it."

I kept 16-millimeter copies of all my films. I had THE BLOB messengered to the beach house, and with my in-house projector, held

Family tower: Grandpa Benny, Father Jack, son Anthony and first grandchildren, Jonathan and Jason Sinay in Malibu, 1965.

a screening for Larry and his family. He hadn't said a word all day. When the screening was over he said, "That fuckin' movie still holds up. How come you never made a sequel?"

I answered, "I believe THE BLOB did all it could do. I was on to other things."

Larry said, "Ain't nothin' you've done that's better than THE BLOB. Goodnight folks."

A few days later, my son Anthony, my Father, and I were chatting. My Father said to Anthony, "Can you imagine it took your Father until this week to show Larry Hagman THE BLOB?" He even suggested a sequel.

I said, "Now he can never say he hasn't seen it." But a fire was ignited under my son who said, "Suppose I get together with Larry and work out a deal to get all of his pals to be in a picture for guild minimum. Would you finance it?"

I said, "You talk to Larry and come back with a proposal. I'll give it serious consideration."

Within a week, Anthony and Larry sat down with me and told me that Carol Lynley, Burgess Meredith, Shelly Berman, Dick Van Patten and Godfrey Cambridge had agreed to appear in the picture if Larry would direct. This last codicil scared the socks off of me. I was afraid he'd make it too funny and not scary enough.

Remembering my promise to Jennifer Jones, I suggested to Larry, now the director of SON OF BLOB, and Anthony, its producer, that we hire Robert Walker, Jr. for the male lead.

Larry said, "Bobby! Great. Why didn't I think of that? "

He got the part.

I'll admit that I was seduced by the name cast at a bargain. I set up the production with Tim Barr, who had supervised the DINOSAURUS and PARADISIO special effects.

During casting, after catching Cindy Williams on a stand-up comedy TV segment, I suggested that the part for the girlfriend to the Carol

Lynley character could be expertly played by Cindy. She was delighted, and we were delighted. She went on to become an even bigger star as Shirley of *Laverne and Shirley.*

I knew my buddy, Richard Clair, had written the aforementioned spec treatment he called, A CHIP OFF THE OL' BLOB. I had earlier rejected it as cute, but too funny and not scary enough. I acquired the script from Richard, and it became the basis of the SON OF BLOB shooting script. In our final conference before shooting started, I had everyone stand and repeat after me, "SON OF BLOB shall be scary and not funny." I forgot to have them swear, because the resulting movie was damned entertaining, but too funny and not scary enough. We were, however, offered rich distribution deals at three different studios. For better or worse, I was so high on the picture that I kept SON OF BLOB for my own distribution company. Anthony, in reviewing his experience as a movie producer, decided it was a dog's life and he was sorry to have temporarily left the music field for it and rushed back to it.

His honesty bowled me over. I couldn't fail to agree.

While the movie world may have lost the talents of my son, the music world gained a gifted musician and composer. With a Masters from USC, Anthony was snapped up by the library and research departments of Frank Sinatra's entourage.

Anthony has been the creator of musical scores for many theatrical feature films, working several times with John Cassavetes: creating the musical scores for his films, MAIN EVENT and KILLER OF A CHINESE BOOKIE.

His ability to play sixteen different instruments makes Anthony a one-man orchestra, though he prefers conducting a real one. Anthony has also penned and produced dozens of commercial themes and remains to this day an in-demand jingle creator.

By mid 1971, SON OF BLOB was completed and in editing. We were celebrating with a cocktail party on Burgess Meredith's deck at Malibu Colony Beach. When Burgess' phone rang, it was a message for Robert Walker Jr. from his mother, Jennifer Jones. Robert would talk, and then repeat to us what was being said. It was Jennifer's second day on the Norton Simon yacht. We said to Bobby, "Did he pop the question?"

He promptly asked, "Mom, did he pop the question?"

Jennifer told him, "I can share the answer with you. It must remain top secret until we announce it. I'm about to become Mrs. Norton Simon."

Robert swore us all to secrecy before divulging the news and then we cracked open a couple of bottles of champagne to celebrate. The news became public about five days later.

⌘

Chapter 15: Beach Neighbors

My neighbor to the south turned out to be a longhaired, bearded, hyper-kinetic charmer named Jon Peters. He and his wife, actress Leslie Ann Warren, and their young son Christopher, helped me pass many pleasant hours in Malibu. Jon was a big name hairdresser and Leslie was coming off of six episodes of "Mission: Impossible." This was after having distinguished herself on Broadway as the title character in CINDERELLA, a role she later repeated on national television.

Jon and I met one morning when I passed him sitting on his beach steps, and he said, "Hi."

I said, "Howdy," and we introduced ourselves.

He asked, "Where are you going?"

"For a walk."

He went on, "Do you need company?"

I responded, "Why not?"

We ambled from the colony beach to the public beach near the Malibu Pier and even as far as Carbon Beach, further south. In that five-mile walk, he asked me more questions about the movie business than a prying district attorney asks of their suspect.

I answered with candor. As we were approaching our respective homes, I told him how much I enjoyed meeting him and walking with him.

He said, "Do you want to know why I asked you all those questions?

I was naturally curious.

He stated, "I've been observing you for a couple of weeks and I've watched you sitting in the sun on your deck, constantly on the telephone making deals and interrupting yourself occasionally for a quick, cooling dip in the Pacific. I've decided whatever you do, I want to do what you do. You're my new idol."

I was flattered, and had no idea at the time that was exactly what he would do. He was one to always learn quickly from those around him.

A couple of weeks later, Jon and Leslie threw a big open house and about 100 people showed up. I was in the living room and Jon came over. He wanted to make sure I was comfortable and having a good time. We got to talking.

He suggested, "Let's go outside."

We went out on the deck to continue our discussion, which was me teaching Jon the rudiments of movie production and distribution. We sat there for almost an hour and the questions were unstoppable. We looked up when we heard, "Well!"

The normally docile Leslie Ann Warren was standing before us breathing fire from her nose and saying, "Maybe you two girls can break this up. There's a party going on and there's no host."

I said, "Jon, I think you should go back inside." I went across the deck back to my home. The lesson was over.

Jon was not my only disciple from his family. Five-year-old Christopher Peters would sneak over to our deck every time his mom and dad were away pursuing their careers. The kid was a charming imp. I got a big kick out of him and he was happy in my company. He soon added joining me for breakfast to this visiting routine, much to my delight. My grandsons, Jonathan and Jason, would show up on weekends, and I'd have a ball with the three of them.

About a year and a half into my friendship with Jon, we were taking a beach walk together. He said to me, "Don't be shocked, but I think Leslie and I have gone as far as we can go together."

I spent the remaining hour of our walk trying to reason with Jon about keeping the family together. He was adamant. He loved Leslie, but he felt that he had more things to do with his life and had to be free.

The Peters family moved from Malibu and pursued their divorce. After awhile, Jon was cutting my hair one day and told me he had a new love in his life.

I asked, "Do I know her?"

He said, "Well, you may not have met her, but you know her."

"Who's that?"

He said, "Her first name is Barbra – with one 'a' missing."

I thought, *Could it be Streisand?*

As if reading my mind, he said, "Bingo."

I asked how it came about.

He explained to me, "A couple of months ago I was asked to do her hair for a new picture, FOR PETE'S SAKE. I showed up at her house promptly and waited in the entrance hall for almost an hour. I lost it. I walked into her secretary's office and said, 'Nobody has the audacity to keep me waiting. I don't care if she's the biggest star in the world. Tell her to find somebody else.' I turned around and almost knocked over the star herself, who was quietly standing in the doorway listening to my tirade."

Barbra had told him, "I'm so sorry. I got into a meeting with my business manager that was supposed to be over an hour before you showed up."

Jon told her, "I hope you heard everything, because I meant every word of it. You can't treat people like dogs."

He explained to me that he then pushed her out of his way and started toward the entrance hall. She went after him and said, "I'm sorry, I'm sorry. What do you want me to do? I'm sorry. I'll make it up to you."

Jon told me, "I calmed down and said, 'do you promise never to do this again to me or anybody else?'"

She said, "I'll promise anything and I mean it."

Jon continued, "I stayed and coiffed the star's hair. As I was finishing, she said, 'Please stay for dinner, and let's get to know each other.'"

Jon thought, "Why the hell not? We became fast friends and have been together ever since." Jon and Barbra decided to buy a Malibu property and build a house.

As he completed this story, I was non-plussed but happy that my friend seemed romantically fulfilled.

A few days later, early on a Sunday morning, Jon called me and he said, "Jackie, there's a friend of mine that would like to talk to you." The next voice I heard was Barbra Streisand saying, "Hello Jack, I've heard so much about you that I feel I know you. It's about time we met."

Before I could answer she said, "Our house is a mess! Why don't Jon and I come over to your house and have brunch together? I'll bring the lox."

I told her, "We have lox and we have two empty chairs for the two of you. Get your asses over here because I'm hungry."

I told my wife Muriel, that we were having a couple of surprise guests for lunch. She said, "I'm glad you're telling me about it after they're invited."

I told her, "There's always plenty of food in the house and this is where we entertain. What difference does it make?"

She exclaimed, "But Barbra Streisand! I'm not even dressed."

I told her not to worry about getting dressed, "Put your face on and comb your hair."

Within an hour, Jon ushered Barbra to our kitchen entrance into the beach house. Barbra was dressed in suitable attire, a bathing suit under a cover up with her hair tied up, she wore minimum make-up. That's all that was necessary with those gorgeous, purple blue eyes and that porcelain skin commanding attention. She was simply attired and very down to earth. She soon put Muriel at ease. Muriel wore a simple caftan and her usual beach necklace, which consisted of a pendant that was really a cocktail glass suspended from her neck. This was the glass she used for many swilling days with Larry Hagman.

The brunch went swimmingly. Who wouldn't be captivated by one of the brightest shining stars in the Hollywood firmament? This began a routine of weekly Sunday get-togethers, where Barbra spent a lot of time with Muriel, discussing her decorating plans. It turns out they were both born under the sign of Taurus and had a simpatico relationship.

Most Sundays we were visited by a series of famous personalities, not the least of which was then Governor Jerry Brown. Jon and I would get the biggest kick out of Barbra arguing politics with the Governor of California.

Every time they were invited to a party elsewhere on the Colony Beach, they were sure to stop by, even just to say, "Hello."

⌘

Chapter 16: Bachelorhood

In 1973, I was invited to bring SON OF BLOB to the San Sebastian Film Festival. During the second day of the festival, I was a guest at the luncheon for a new Carlo Ponti production, THE VOYAGE, starring Sophia Loren and Richard Burton. When the luncheon speeches were over, the crowd mobbed Sophia and Richard. I was standing alone, except for a cute little guy standing next to me who happened to be Carlo Ponti. I shook his hand and introduced myself. He said he heard of THE BLOB and hoped the sequel would be just as successful.

I congratulated him on his series of memorable productions, which had been a tutorial for me in Italian cinema. They had really blazed the way for the internationalization of Italian films. I was effusive about THE VOYAGE and he said, "It's a small, but honest film which was intended for television. It's getting away from us and will be shown theatrically." He was animated, lively, and utterly charming. I was so happy that I wound up with him instead of the two stars.

Richard looked like he had to go to the bathroom. Sophia kept a steady, quiet gaze on Carlo all through our conversation.

Coincidentally, I met a young, tall, red-headed American television distributor at the festival named Ben Barry. Ben and I hit it off well. I taught him how to play backgammon, and he taught me a lot about what was going on in TV distribution. We remain friends to this day, although his hair has turned white and mine is still mostly black.

My Father, back in Philly, continued his distribution business armed with the remnants of the theatrical titles I bestowed upon him when I closed my Philadelphia distribution office.

Larry and Maj Hagman surprised him in early 1973 by dropping in on his Vine Street office during a trip to New York. Upon their return to Malibu they told me he was so happy for their visit. Sadly, they expressed concern for how much he had deteriorated physically since they last saw him in Malibu.

I immediately telephoned my sister Dotzie. She verified that our Father was having breathing problems. I suspected his tired heart.

Dotzie and her husband Frank Gorman had convinced Father to take a week off and spend it with them at their Broomall, Pennsylvania house. He complained to me in daily phone calls that if he could only sleep better, he'd feel better. One day in March, 1973, he complained that he was feeling miserable. The next day my sister tearfully telephoned me with the news of my Father's sudden death at the age of seventy-five.

There was a reading of his will, which began, "I am eternally grateful for the success and business acumen of my dear son, Jack H. Harris. He has acquired substantial equities and, therefore, will be pleased to know that my estate shall herewith be exclusively bequeathed to my three beloved daughters, Claire, Mitzie and Dotzie."

I was dumbfounded to realize that his bequeathed estate, assembled in no small part by me, failed to include me in its distribution. I was deeply hurt. It was not the equity involved, but the unappreciativeness of it that really disturbed me. I already trusted no one. This confirmed my resolve to do as I wish for others, but never to expect anything in return – not even appreciation.

I forgave my Father years ago, but I've never forgotten.

When I think about how my personal and business relationships may have been influenced by him and our relationship, two things immediately come to mind – trust and respect. These two things have been of utmost importance in every other relationship, as I never shared either with him. If someone crosses me, we're done. I had to keep returning to an unfortunate business and personal relationship with my Father, so never again. But if someone honors their word, we're in business forever.

Out of the blue, I got a strange phone call from an oldish yet naive voice coming out of a young Dennis Muren. He had completed a movie which he called, EQUINOX, THE LINE BETWEEN LIFE AND DEATH, and wanted to discuss distribution with me. I met with him. He showed up at my office on the appointed day. He was a very tall, gangly, nineteen-year-old, who didn't look like he could complete a snapshot, let alone a movie.

I listened to him very carefully as he described his tribulations in getting the movie made. He explained the theme as four teenagers being in a duel with the devil. He really got my attention when he told me about the special effects and the monsters in the production. He had been assisted by Jim Danforth, who had done some work on DINOSAURUS. I was hooked. "Dennis, let me see it," I said.

He said, "I thought you'd never ask," as he pulled a 16-millimeter print of the picture out of his shoulder bag and laid it on my desk. I took the print home that night. After dinner, Muriel and Anthony joined me for a screening of EQUINOX.

Muriel lasted ten minutes and excused herself. Anthony reluctantly stayed with it. I was especially impressed with the special effects sequences showing monsters, devils, and other strange creatures. They were as good as any professional special effects I'd ever seen. My son was totally unimpressed with the film. He found the acting, dialogue, and storyline amateurish and boring. I told him that I agreed with him but I planned to find a way to retain the special effects and reshoot 60% of the movie, blending the new footage into the usable old footage.

The next day I made a deal with Dennis' father to acquire the picture. He seemed pleased to get rid of it. I assumed he had been the financing source.

I called upon a good friend and associate, Jack Woods, to get to the movieola and figure out what we could keep and what we had to lose. The two Jacks had to make a working arrangement. We would be spending about ten hours a day together and Jack Woods was a four packer. I was a never-having-smoked-because-I'm-allergic-to-nicotine-abstainer. We agreed on fifty-minute non-smoking hours, separated by ten minute smoking breaks, during which Jack would imbibe in a well-ventilated, outdoor space.

After about five days of concentrated effort, we at least knew what we had. We also knew what we had to get. Jack also was elated to discover that he could go fifty smoke-free minutes on a continuing basis. He could even forego, toward the end of our schedule, a few of his ten-minute smoking breaks. Unwittingly, I had induced him to ultimately quit smoking.

Jack and I designed an overall structure. We rehired the original cast and during a ten-day schedule were able to complete the re-shooting, working off of a script written and directed by Jack Woods. We also cast Jack Woods as the horseback-riding ranger named Asmodeus, another name for the devil.

After the completion of Post Production, Jack Woods and I screened the rough cut. Out of the four actors in the original, Frank Bonner Jr., who went on to a fine career in television including *WKRP In Cincinnati*, was the only decent voice performance. The other actors were re-voiced during a six-day looping schedule at MGM Studios by Joanie Gerber, doing both girls, and announcer, Larry Burrell, doing the male lead. Thanks to the very talented supervision of Jack Woods, this new soundtrack blended seamlessly into the finished product. This made that finished product into a first class, professional film.

We sneak previewed EQUINOX at the Hollywood Theatre on Hollywood Boulevard. At the end of the picture there was audience applause. My son said to me, "Dad, you performed a miracle. I was really terrified, the picture has a suspense quality."

The movie went on to great box office success and became a cult classic. Dennis, the young filmmaker, went on to work for George Lucas and became his special effects supervisor, ultimately winning nine Academy Awards.

I consider it great kismet and a great pleasure of mine to have been able to cross paths with some very talented filmmakers at the beginning of their careers. Hopefully, I gave them the sort of assistance or wisdom that I might not have had access to when I was starting out. When I look at their successes, and their excellent films, I can only hope that I had some humble, positive influence or affect on this creative Hollywood lineage and the wonderful tradition of cinema.

Another one of these encounters began when an attorney friend, Herb Nusbaum, brought a young, hopeful filmmaker, John Landis, to meet with me. John, had written, produced, and starred in a really nutty personal production under the title, SCHLOCK. SCHLOCK, the lead played by John Landis, was a prehistoric missing link, which the scientists in the movie called, Schlockthropous. The character had wandered from the jungle into today's society and created havoc whenever modern man displeased him. Since it dealt with a simian monster, I was fascinated, but it needed some beefing up. It was not quite sixty-minutes long and contained some hilarious moments. John and I put together a theatre sequence where SCHLOCK takes my grandson, Jason, to see a double feature of THE BLOB and DINOSAURUS. During the shooting of this sequence, the audience (containing my daughter, Lynda, her new boyfriend, Stewart Resnick, and his three children) played movie watchers who were greatly disturbed by the antics of The Schlock in their midst. The monster threw popcorn all over one of the patrons. When his view of the screen was obscured by a lady wearing a large hat, the monster removed it only to find that her springy hair was taller than the hat. So, he proceeded to eat the hat.

John Landis in the Schlock suit APE-ing it up with Jack H. Harris.

In another scene, my six-year-old grandson, Jason, sitting next to Schlock, had the urge to urinate and asked Schlock to take him to the restroom. There's a hilarious scene with Schlock leading Jason by the hand to show him where the men's room is located. It took just one long day to shoot the sequence, giving us a much needed, fifteen-minute segment.

When SCHLOCK was finished, I held a trade screening and none of the exhibitors got very excited. My next plan was to release SON OF BLOB and SCHLOCK to principally drive-in theatres with a big campaign in the Greater Los Angeles Area. To my great satisfaction, both pictures got terrific reviews from L.A. columnist, Kevin Thomas, which helped a lot. Later, both pictures separately won a Grand Prix at the San Sebastian science-fiction film festival in Italy. Neither picture broke any box office records. Ultimately, they were just nice titles to have on the release chart.

SCHLOCK also did just mildly in VHS. Sometime in the '70s, I gave the picture back to John Landis. His career had taken off with ANIMAL HOUSE, BLUES BROTHERS and a couple of Eddie Murphy movies.

He still hasn't had time to do anything much with SCHLOCK.

While the SCHLOCK business was wrapping up, my secretary kept reminding me that I hadn't returned several telephone calls from a student filmmaker named John Carpenter. She explained that he had a new science fiction film available for distribution. I talked to Carpenter, who came to my office with his partner, Dan O'Bannon. They were seniors at USC and would shortly be graduating from the film school there. They had completed a sci-fi movie called, DARK STAR, that seemed like a turn-off title to me.

I screened the picture. The opening scene showed a space ship orbiting heavenly bodies in deep, deep, deep space. Cut to one of the astronauts going into a room and mumbling something about being very tired. He climbs into a bunk. The camera dollies back to show about eight others in various stages of sleep on their bunks. The scene went on for eight minutes without a word of dialogue. It was just sounds of snoring. I sat through ninety-minutes of this amateurish attempt, but was turned on by various episodes in the piece that showed sheer brilliance and tremendous creativity.

I sat down with the boys and worked out a deal where I would advance the funds necessary to recut and eliminate the unreleaseable portions, replacing them with action and mixing them with other useable footage. I guaranteed the return of their investment and we would split the profits after recoupment.

DARK STAR is the story of a space ship by that name in the future with a mission to destroy unstable planets so they would not endanger Planet Earth.

John Carpenter turned out to be a first-class director and turned this picture into a classic. His career has been outstanding, and has included iconic titles such as HALLOWEEN, THE THING, and THE FOG. Dan O'Bannon, who wrote the screenplay, went on to do ALIEN and other pictures of the genre.

I sold DARK STAR to Bryanston Films for a decent profit above our costs and settled up with the boys. I regret walking away from the picture, which went on to become an international icon.

At this point in my life, my ailing marriage to Muriel had been unraveling for years. Her smoking intensified, lighting each new cigarette with the burning butt of the current one. Her alcohol intake increased daily, difficult for a non-smoker, light drinker like me. She offered to relocate to a separate bed and bath.

This went on for years until our children were on their own. Our divorce was inevitable, finally taking place formally in 1974. We equally shared our joint property. The emotional toll of it all rendered me lacking in energy and spirit. Many, including our children, were surprised that it had taken us so long to divorce.

I gave the beach house to Muriel in the divorce settlement. I bought two apartments and began living in one at the Outrigger, a forty-four-unit condominium security building on Carbon Beach in Malibu. My most frequent guests were Jon and Barbra, and every time they would come to visit it would stop traffic. I had a very glamorous two-bedroom, two-bath, 2,500 square foot unit with the beach/ocean surrounding my location on three sides. We spent many enjoyable hours together on my deck and in my home. I guess my tutelage to Jon had worked, because he now had become Barbra's producer.

Eventually, tennis and TV star, Vince Van Patten and his friend, Farrah Fawcett dropped in on one of my gatherings and were smitten by my elegant unit. Farrah was particularly impressed with the beachfront ambiance, living quarter appointments, and total privacy. She asked, "Would you ever sell it?"

"Sure," I casually replied. "But it would take a good price to evict me from these digs." She turned to Vince with, "You're looking for a beach home. How can you beat this?"

Vince was silently searching for words when I eased him up with, "Think it over, Vince. Let me know if you're serious. This place is not on the market, but I could be motivated as I own another nearby unit and could move there easily."

Two days later, Dick Van Patten, Vince's dad, called me for an appointment to see my apartment. He met me, briefcase in hand, at my office, located directly across Pacific Coast Highway from the Outrigger building. We crossed the street together, giving him a full treatment approach to the beach building, the entrance, and on to the private hallway to my apartment front door.

I unlocked the door and held it open for him to behold the 180-degree view of the Pacific Ocean, visible through the continuous picture windows. Dick was visibly affected. He could only say, "Jack, this is nice. Now I know why Vince is so impressed."

We went over to the bar and I relieved him of his suitcase. We were soon sipping drinks, admiring the view and reminiscing about his very funny cameo appearance during the shooting of SON OF BLOB. He got right back to business with, "How much are you asking?"

"Dick," I answered, "I'm not asking anything. If your son wants to buy this place it will cost him $800,000 dollars."

Dick started fishing in his briefcase for something and stated, "I was prepared to offer $650,000, but I'll go to $700,000."

I told him, "It will cost $800,000 to evict me from this wonderful, completely remodeled dwelling place."

He looked hurt, but I smiled. "We're still good buddies, even if he doesn't buy it, so don't feel so bad."

Then he surprised me with, "OK, it's a deal."

That's the way the purchase/escrow was inaugurated. Farrah, it turned out was the happiest of this cast of characters.

One Saturday, a week or so later, there was a knock at my door. This was a security building and nobody could get to my door unless they lived in the building. I opened the door and saw Mel Brooks grinning at me, putting his hand out for a shake and saying, "Hello, Jack, may I come in." I bade him welcome and he was followed by Anne Bancroft, Carl and Estelle Reiner, Dick Van Patten and his lovely wife, Pat, and Joan Fontaine.

Dick said, "I hope you don't mind. I was just describing your house and my pals all voiced the curiosity to view it. After the introductions, I began to show them around. We all gathered in the master bedroom at the main picture window and I suddenly snapped the drapes open to gasps of appreciation. Carl Reiner, closest to the window noticed a garden party in full swing just below and announced, "Ladies and gentlemen, good afternoon. Mr. Harris wanted us to say hello to you. Let me introduce beautiful and glamorous Anne Bancroft. Come here, Anne." She walked past the window slowly smiling and bowing to the applause below. Carl resumed, "Now Joan Fontaine, come on Joan, leading Pat Van Patten across the window. "Oh yes," said Carl, "Here's Dick Van Patten." Dick stood at the window waving silent thank yous to the crowd, then left. "And, my beautiful wife," said Carl, leading Estelle to the window, as she sang a line from "Tiptoe Through the Tulips." Then she exited.

"Oh," continued Carl, "I almost forgot, here's the 2000 year old man, Mel Brooks, in person. Mel ambled slowly past the window throwing huge kisses. Carl stood there and asked, "Have you seen enough stars?" The crowd roared approval. Carl answered, "Thank you, next show 8:00 PM." He snapped the curtain quickly closed.

I got hugs and kisses from the ladies and warm, buddy handshakes from the guys as they exited quickly amid "thank yous."

My next revelation may not sound very Hollywoodish. I was a bachelor who wasn't out to "nail" everything that walked.

I dated a few ladies and was smitten with budding actress/model, Nancy Fitzgerald, age twenty-one, who moved in with me. The difference between her and my glamour gals was refreshing, and we spontaneously married. I soon realized how difficult our relationship became. I was fifty-eight and we called it quits after five months. It was a mutually agreeable dissolution.

I remained a bachelor until I was sixty-four and met beauteous socialite Barbara Weiss, her two children, and her four saddle-bred horses. I was most flattered that she left her husband to marry me, until I signed the wedding document and realized I was "number five." It took less than two years for a divorce to be looming, but it took about ten months to get that divorce because the billionaire heiress tried to take all of my equity to add to her fortune. Fortunately, I had an excellent attorney, Neil Hersh, who was aided by the fact that Barbara met another guy and aborted the marriage.

⌘

Chapter 17: Eyes of Laura Mars

I enjoyed my relationship with Jon Peters. Jon was a good pal, and in spite of his youth, a very savvy student of life. He'd been married for the first time at the age of sixteen. His relationship with Barbra Streisand continued apace. They were designing houses, tennis courts, swimming pools, and other accoutrements at their Malibu ranch. They had the remake of A STAR IS BORN on Barbra's plate. In spite of all the lovey-dovey stories in the press about bringing their romance into the plot and Jon directing the picture, there was one major problem. Barbra wouldn't commit to the production.

Warner Brothers was backing the film and were absolutely at wits end to get a start date. They thoroughly believed in the project, yet Barbra wouldn't commit.

One day, Jon and I were lunching at the studio commissary and he sat there with tears in his eyes saying, "Why the fuck won't she commit? We can get this multi-million dollar picture made and my producer career can get started."

"Jon," I said, "I have the solution, if you will listen to me and do as I say, she'll commit."

He sat and looked at me very seriously, "What's your solution?"

I said, "She loves you madly and would do anything for you, but the professional side of her existence is at stake. You have no idea what you'd be in for if you directed the picture. I did it once. I'd never do it again. Just simply say, 'Barbra, I withdraw as director of the picture,' let's get it made.'"

He looked at me, blinked his eyes and said, "OK, I'll do it."

The next day the picture was set and Barbra was committed. The trades heralded the story, "Barbra agrees to do A STAR IS BORN."

In 1974, John Carpenter wrote an eleven-page treatment for a film called EYES, which I agreed to produce as a feature film. It was the story of a fashion photographer/protagonist who would at times lose her vision and see murders being committed through the eyes of a total stranger. I had decided to go the non-studio route and wound up with featured player, Roberta Collins, in the key role with the financing coming from the private sector. My approach was low-key and low-cost.

I was sitting in my office and working on ideas for the writing of the screenplay when Jon Peters opened the door and said, "Hello, Jackie, what are you working on?"

I showed him Carpenter's eleven-pages and explained my production approach. He looked over the pages and said, "Do you know what you've got here?"

I answered, "Yes, the basis of one hell of a movie."

Jon went on, "You've got the basis of a major movie starring Barbra Streisand in the kind of role she's never played."

I said, "Jon, my deal is set. My next step is getting the screenplay done so we can schedule a start date for the picture."

He said, "Hold everything. Give me two days. I'll get you Barbra and Columbia Studios to back the picture." He grabbed my eleven pages and was out the door before I could even answer.

I had been around the pike a few times and had heard all kinds of things, and I knew that he was whistling Dixie. Three hours later, Peter Guber, then assistant head of production at Columbia, got me on the phone with the most positive reaction I'd ever seen for one of my projects. He had chills at the right time and tears at the right time. He was anxious to get the project underway as soon as possible. He thought Barbra would be an Oscar contender in the part. I immediately cancelled my independent preparation for the project.

Jon and I made a deal with John Carpenter to write the screenplay and participate in the profits. As the written pages started developing they were pure gold, and our discussions with Barbra were going amazingly well. Jon came up with the brilliant suggestion to make the killer the detective "trying" to solve the murders. Jon and Barbra were in the middle of shooting A STAR IS BORN during this period. It was wonderful that either of them had the time to be enthusiastic about EYES.

The screenplay was completed and being analyzed by Columbia Pictures. We were confident that the screenplay did great justice to the eleven-page treatment, of which Carpenter delivered page twelve to us just as we were going into production. Imagine being able to finance a feature deal based on eleven pages of a twelve-page treatment.

That night I was awakened at 1:30 AM with a call from Barbra Streisand. She sounded very teary.

I asked, "Honey, is there some trouble?"

She said, "Yes, dear, there's a lot of trouble. I have been so concerned about doing a horror movie. I went to sleep with that on my mind and just awoke from a terrible nightmare that shattered me. I told Jon I would have to bow out of the picture, and he said I should call you immediately."

Knowing Barbra pretty well by now, I could only say, "Barbra, could you give it some further consideration and think about it in the morning?"

She said, "Jack, darling, there isn't anything in the world I wouldn't do for you, but please don't make me live up to my commitment to star in this picture. I just can't do it."

I said, "Very well, I won't pressure you any further, but I do appreciate your prompt timing and your candid expression."

I was crestfallen because I knew that Barbra, then at the peak of her powerful career, would have made this a movie that would sail to the top of the grossing charts and also be an irrefutably gripping experience for the moviegoers. The next day, bright and early, we let Columbia know of the turn of events. They were so committed to the screenplay that they said "Let's find another actress."

Faye Dunaway had just won the Academy Award for her performance in NETWORK, and we duly pursued her to assay the part. A deal was struck in a couple of days, and we moved into studio mandated screen-play rewrites. Time was going by as we went through the efforts of five notable writers. I felt we were getting nowhere, but Jon felt otherwise. After we had finished the fifth rewrite, I talked to Roz Heller, who was our studio executive on the picture and said, "We've guaranteed a budget, and we're already into five rewrites. I think if we go back and examine the original, it was pretty close to being there."

Roz said, "Nonsense. We're not even up to half a million dollars on the writing budget yet. Don't get hysterical."

We signed David Z. Goodman, Oscar-nominee for LOVERS AND OTHER STRANGERS, to do what we thought was going to be the final rewrite and started again. After his pass, everyone agreed to greenlight the project. We knuckled down to serious pre-production. The first jolt we got was when we registered the title, EYES, to discover that there was a short story by the same name already in publication.

We changed the title to EYES OF LAURA MARS, and featured the title with the word "EYES" at 75% and the balance at 15%. The cast and crew moved to New York City to begin shooting the Manhattan locations. David Z. Goodman was assigned to keep rewriting as we were shooting. Unbeknownst to me, Jon had promised Faye Dunaway that she would have a voice in the writing of the final screenplay. Faye stopped talking to Jon, which made for a less than happy set. On one of his quick weekend trips to Los Angeles, I went over to Faye's apartment, which was in the next building to Barbra Streisand's penthouse where Jon and I were staying. We discussed the problem.

I said, "Jon is a very enthusiastic guy. He thinks the world of you and is very hurt that you are not communicating with him."

Faye said, "I've been lied to. Shooting is scheduled to start, and I have not attended one writing session."

I told her that I would make arrangements for her to attend the remaining sessions whenever her schedule permitted. She hugged and kissed me and promised to forgive Jon.

She went to David Z. Goodman's apartment, and director Irvin Kershner was also there. Irvin told me that Faye arrived in the biggest limousine he had ever seen, and sat through the whole three-hour script session sipping wine and making comments. Jon returned to the set two days later, and it was lovey-dovey again between him and Faye.

During the fourth week of production, I made a deal with the Rolex Company to support the release of the picture provided Faye Dunaway wore their watch during shooting. She said nothing to me about the matter, but called the head of the studio, Dan Melnick, telling him that Jack Harris was turning her into a commercial model and that's beneath her stature as a movie star. She threatened to walk off the picture.

Dan called me and angrily related what Faye had told him. I said, "Dan, we probably could have gotten a half a million dollars in promotional subsidy out of the Rolex Company. If she doesn't want to do it, time marches on anyway. What's the big deal?"

He said, "Let her wear any watch she wants to."

I said, "Done."

My relationship with Faye cooled until a few days later when she was sitting behind me at a screening of dailies and goosed me when I stood up and she said, "Let's see you laugh, you crabby bastard."

What could I do? I laughed.

Jon Peters and I each did our work on the picture, but when it came to credit or visibility, he was very astute at seeing that I got little or none of the above. Doing the picture was a humbling experience for me.

During production, Jon ran back and forth to the west coast, sometimes missing half a week of shooting problems and straining the fragile budget we had guaranteed with the studio. On one of his quick forays to the New York shoot, he came upon me yelling, "Mr. Executive Producer, you did it again."

I was a bit startled and said, "What are you talking about?"

He said, "One of the huge photo blow-ups in our photographic exhibition set shows Lisa Taylor with her boobs bared."

I wondered how that reflected on me since I neither selected the pictures nor shot them. I said, "It's a nice picture, and it reflects the facts of a model's life."

Jon attacked me with, "You should have read her contract."

I asked him how many of the contracts we generated for the picture he read.

"That's not the point," he yelled. "We got a problem, she's going to sue us for showing her bare boobs in the scenes which included the photo blow-up."

"Jon," I said, "you don't know when to stop. This is the first I know of the problem. Since you can't, I'll resolve it." I took Lisa out to lunch and discussed it with her.

She declared, "I want to cooperate and I understand the difficulty of your position. I'll do anything reasonable to resolve the matter."

I told her to leave it to me. I went and sat with Michael Kind, the editor. We reviewed the scene and using the old 'Vaseline on the lens' trick, we were able to reduce her likeness to an indiscernible image in the final context of the scene. When it was all over, I went to Jon who was sitting with Laura Ziskin, our assistant, and told him the problem had been handled.

He didn't say "Thanks. I'm sorry I got tough with you." Or anything else except, "That's nice."

I said to Jon, "You're an obnoxious prick."

He giggled and kissed me. Laura looked suitably startled.

I made up my mind that the next picture I did with Jon would be far in the future, if at all.

Off the set we had some good times. One night Barbra, Jon, agent Sue Mengers, and Jon's son Christopher invited me to dinner at a Japanese restaurant, after which we would all walk over to 42nd Street for the premiere of the live theatre performance of DRACULA, with Frank Langella assaying the title role. During dinner, Chris sat next to me, as usual. I asked him if he had seen the old movie DRACULA starring Bela Lugosi. "No," the seven-year-old replied, "but I read the book." All assembled cracked up.

EYES OF LAURA MARS was wrapped, screened and made ready for the marketplace. During this time, Faye Dunaway had found a copy of a highbrow German photography magazine, on the cover of which was a serious looking character with streams of light emanating from his eyes. We all thought it would make a cute trade paper ad to let the exhibitors know the picture was completed and on its way. Our ad showed Faye in a very dark frame, with streams of light coming from her eyes. The exhibitor response was overwhelmingly positive, so much so that try as I might to dissuade the distribution department from keeping this image as the key art for the public, they would not change the campaign. I felt it was too dark and too off-putting. We did have a very memorable and well-done thriller.

Barbra and her son, Jason, arrived from California to be in New York for the completion of production. I had moved to the Lombardy Hotel. One night I was invited to dinner by Barbra. She and Jon sat at the dining table with me. We had a fun time dissing Hollywood. When coffee was served, Barbra asked me to help her edit an interview she gave to Playboy Magazine. It was about twenty-five pages of copy, which she pleaded with me to evaluate and offer suggestions. It turned into a six-hour session. Jon had retired at 10:30 PM, and she caught me yawning and excused me at 3:00 AM. Barbra walked me to the door and gave me a nice, big kiss goodnight and thanked me profusely for making the interview terrific.

Two days later at their house, Jon and I had a production meeting with Irvin Kirshner on EYES OF LAURA MARS, which broke up about 11:00 PM. As I was saying goodnight, Barbra, article in hand, asked Irvin to help her edit the Playboy Magazine interview. Jon whispered to me that I was the tenth expert that had helped her with it.

EYES OF LAURA MARS opened to great reviews and mediocre business, to everybody's astonishment. Although the studio allowed me to work up an alternative campaign, in the days of mass marketing, it was too little, too late. The picture had a successful life in VHS and DVD distribution. Everyone I meet or know tells me about how fantastic the picture was, leaving me puzzled as to whether they had actually seen the picture, or simply remembered Faye Dunaway and the streaming-light eyes key art.

During the third week of shooting, I was invited to the premiere party for CLOSE ENCOUTERS OF THE THIRD KIND, a memorable Steven Spielberg film. After the preview of the picture, we all went to the Tavern on the Green, which was taken over for the party and closed to the public that night. I found myself seated a table away from Jacqueline Kennedy, who at the time was editor for a publishing company. She was in conversation with Pete Hamill, her then steady, when I went over to chat with her.

Pete stood up and offered, "Take my seat."

What do you talk to Jackie Kennedy about? I quickly discarded politics, children, and other controversial subjects. I asked her how it felt to be in her editorial position. She was very effusive and pleased to be discussing what she was doing and how she found each day a comfort and satisfaction doing valuable work.

I invited her to the proposed premiere of EYES OF LAURA MARS. She seemed flattered at the advance invitation. I asked, "Will you come?"

She replied, "If you invite me."

I sat looking at Jackie with pleasant thoughts. She was, indeed, a beautiful woman. Desire was not part of my thinking. Being able to be in the presence of such an outstanding woman was very gratifying to me.

She was one of the nicest, most genuine people I've ever had the good fortune to meet.

As things turned out, my daughter and her new husband were giving a black and white ball at their mansion on Sunset Blvd., in Beverly Hills the exact same night as our movie premiere party in New York. Lynda had me on the phone for an hour pleading with me to be by her side when her party took place.

I explained to Jon that I wouldn't be at the premiere party because of my obligation to my daughter, and asked him to be kind to Jacqueline Kennedy in my absence. He gallantly promised he would.

I enjoyed my daughter's party very much and was very proud of her and her second husband, Stewart Resnick. Together they had become a social and business success, and I was glad to see how they were getting along. Of course, I missed the premiere, but in thinking back on it, I made the right decision.

The Resnicks have just celebrated their forty-second anniversary. Together they have created an extraordinary empire including TELEFLORA, FIJI WATER, POM WONDERFUL and a cornucopia of the fruits and nuts from their fields. Their philanthropy has earned them the title of "Rockefellers of L.A." Lynda's book *Rubies in the Orchard: The Pom Queen's Secrets to Marketing Just About Anything,* the story of POMegranate juice, appeared on Amazon.com as a National Bestseller.

⌘

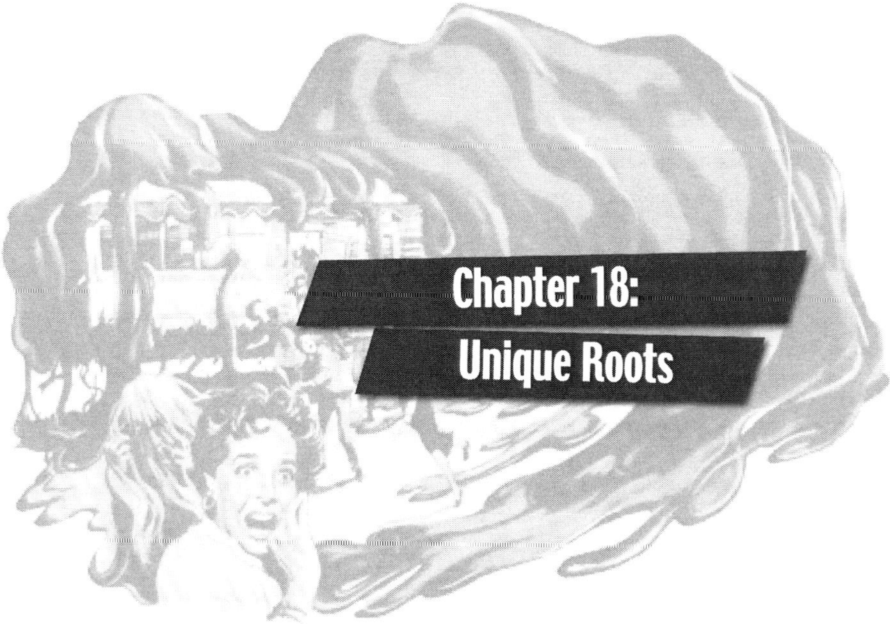

Chapter 18: Unique Roots

In the days of the Hayes Office in the 1930s, through the vigilance of the Catholic Church with their *Legion of Decency,* even to and including the present Motion Picture Association ratings system, the movies have been constantly attacked on sexual content and explicit violence. Television has had to deal with public and private censorship, too. Book publishing has also been harassed by similar censoring bodies.

Bernard Rossett, head of Grove Press, a small but vital publishing company, happened to discover, while in the Royal Albert Museum in London, an anonymous manuscript entitled, MY SECRET LIFE. The manuscript detailed a wealthy English gentleman's obsession with sexuality. Although this manuscript was published in the early 19th century, it was un-copyrighted and therefore in the public domain. Bernard was probably not the first to discover the manuscript, but he was the first to announce the publication of it. Advance copies of the resultant book were viciously attacked by church and public groups.

This wound up in an obscenity trial which achieved tremendous public notice. Grove Press was exonerated and the book went on sale to astronomical numbers.

Early in 1971, a young student in the McGill University of Toronto Film School got a copy and decided to direct and produce a film based on the book as his senior thesis. He was able to get Shakespearean actor, Robert Fathergill, to narrate the film. He also corralled a fine cast of young, beautiful people.

Ivan Reitman, the student producer, arranged to show the picture in its rough form at the University auditorium to a standing ovation. Also standing were several members of the Canadian Constabulary with a warrant for his arrest and a confiscation attachment for his film.

I read about the whole fiasco and contacted Ivan, who was released from prison and on probation. He was delighted to hear from me. I flew to Toronto and had a meeting with Ivan, during which we discussed distribution potential. First, I had to see the film.

He bemoaned the fact that his 35 mm version was confiscated, but he still had a 16 mm print in secret storage. We went to a private home with the print and a projector and for eighty-minutes I sat between amazement and jolts as the narration, literally verbatim from the book, described every sex act imaginable in blatant unvarnished colloquial terms. At the end of the screening, I couldn't remember if there were any unsaid obscenities. To this day, I doubt it.

We made a deal. He begged me, because of his censorship experience, not to put his name on the film. Since his name meant nothing at the time, it was easy for me to agree. Now, almost forty years later, I think I've done my share of keeping his name quiet.

The visual portion of this student film varied from amateurish to exceptional. I sat down with my editor Jack Woods, and very carefully deleted the crappy scenes and then wrote some new sequences and shot them in Hollywood. We retained all of the epithet-peppered dialogue, and even added some extra readings from the book. The picture opened on Broadway at the Loews State Theater and played in important theatres in all of the metropolitan areas of the U.S. Grove Press contributed thousands of paperback copies of the book to be handed out to the first fifty patrons of each showing.

It was a success and a real coup to be able to exhibit such a ground-breaking production that presented to the American public for the first time our language, with all of the obscenities fully intact and in place. Strangely, we experienced very little in the way of censorship complaints. Ivan Reitman went on to a successful and prolific career, producing and directing features such as ANIMAL HOUSE, KINDERGARTEN COP, GHOSTBUSTERS and many others.

One day an officious young fellow telephoned me and specifically gave his name to my secretary, "Please tell Mr. Harris that it's Fred Olen Ray calling."

I was busy, but his name made me curious and I took his call. He had an idea for a sci-fi movie and had already shot about twenty minutes of the notion. I asked what his working title was and he said, PRISON SHIP. I asked what it was about, and he said, "Women in prison, in space, in the future." I recalled a movie by that title in the 1930s, which starred Warner Baxter, and had nothing to do with space and hardly anything to do with women. I knew Fred's picture had to establish new ground.

I looked at his reel and was impressed that he was able to do that much with so little cash outlay. He requested that I supply the financing needed to turn the twenty minutes into a ninety-minute feature film. I told him I was interested and had to work out the financial details and would get back to him.

Within a week, Ed Sarlui, a Dutchman who had started an independent distribution company a few years earlier, contacted me. None of his titles were big hits, but they all filled a niche that commanded space on drive-in theatre programming. Ed was a sucker for women's prison pictures, and this idea came along just at the right time. We had a very interesting lunch together, and within ten-minutes of my telling Ed my idea about the women in prison in space in the future, he agreed to split the cost with me on completing the picture.

I had never heard of anyone with a name like his before. He explained that when the Jews arrived in Holland, one of the perks was that they were not allowed a last name. When Napoleon overran and conquered Holland he decreed that all Jews without last names should assume as their last name the name of the town they were born in. Ed's ancestors were born in Sarlui, Holland.

Fred Olen Ray and I worked very closely in planning a production, and he rapidly proved to me his acumen and capability. He enjoyed relationships with some old-timers among which were Aldo Ray and John Carradine, both of whom agreed to do cameos in our picture.

Production took about three months. We were very fortunate to be able to take advantage of several important, about-to-be struck science fiction sets and costumes. With the astute maneuvering of Fred Olen Ray, we brought the picture in on time and under budget. Yet, toward the end of production Ed Sarlui was running out of money, and I graciously bailed him out. My son, Anthony, had done a score for an Indiana Jones-like movie that never happened. We were able to adapt that score with brilliant results. The picture was finished and retitled STAR SLAMMER. It screened up beautifully.

In short order, I made a deal with Trimark Pictures to pay me $75,000 over the budget in return for distribution rights. The picture came along in the waning days of drive-in theatres and was a fair grosser, but has had a good life in VHS and DVD distribution.

Just recently, I got a notice from one of my advisors to call Retro Media, as they were distributing DVD pictures of lesser note than the major studios were providing. I asked for the principal, and Fred Olen Ray got on the phone. It had been twenty years since we had seen each other, and we met and discussed old times and new ones.

Fred now has a thriving DVD distribution company and has made or acquired over thirty films for distribution. We are in discussion about some of my lesser titles for the DVD market.

⌘

Chapter 19: Scaling the Peaks

In 1975, a lady producer I met socially, raved to me about her acquaintance with an agent named Mike Selsman. I hadn't had much need for agents, but several things were cropping up that required that I be able to consult with a reliable, knowledgeable agent, so I contacted Mike.

He came to my bachelor digs in Malibu, and we spent a very friendly hour together discussing some of the things I had on my mind. He offered to be of any help he could, and I found this gratifying. In the late '50s, Mike became personal secretary to Spyros Skouras, a major stockholder of 20th Century Fox, who was in the throes of firing Daryl F. Zanuck, head of the corporation. Spyros was also President of Skouras Theatres, a huge circuit located in the Eastern U.S.

Mike's weekends were taken up by his need to be at Spyro's beck and call at his Long Island Estate. Eventually, Daryl Zanuck was out as head of the studio and sent to France to produce a movie.

Mike moved to Hollywood with Spyros and enjoyed being ensconced at the top level of 20th Century Fox Studios. Spyros championed CinemaScope, a method of shooting and projecting a movie, but met his downfall when he produced CLEOPATRA, starring Elizabeth Taylor, Richard Burton and Rex Harrison. The well-publicized excesses that made the set a romantic playground (Liz cheating on hubby Eddie Fisher with Richard Burton), caused the picture to be the most expensive the studio had ever produced. When CLEOPATRA went out in theatres, it took the good luck of television and ancillary sales many years to finally clear a profit.

When Spyros exited the studio, Mike became part of the publicity department and one of his studio assignments was Carol Lynley. After a whirlwind romance, they married. Their marriage coincided with Carol's reluctance to show up for various films. The studio heads put the screws on Mike to deliver her. He tried to let them know that Carol made up her own mind about her career. Carol took umbrage and told the brass that the reason she wasn't showing up was because her husband Mike was getting in the way. She was divorcing him and suggested they do so as well.

Bewildered and incredulous, Mike took both pink slips with bitterness and proceeded to the independent agency way of life. I've known Mike for thirty years. We have been through a lot together. I have found him to be very astute, very knowledgeable, and a good friend. We eventually got to work together on a proposed remake of THE BLOB, to be done as an animation feature, directed by Ralph Bakshi, of FRITZ THE CAT, a famous animated semi-porn, cartoon.

In 1979, we were set up at the biggest, independent studio in Hollywood, American International Pictures, run by Samuel Z. Arkoff. We held a meeting in Sam's office during which he exuded tremendous enthusiasm for the project and gave it an immediate green light, a rarity in Hollywood.

The very next week, I had to ask Sam a question, and for the first time in the many years I knew him, a week went by and Sam didn't return my call. I was furious and called his assistant and vented upon her. She almost tearfully told me that Sam had been in fifteen-hour meetings with the brass at Filmways, who had merged their company with Sam's. They asserted their prerogative in buying up Sam's stock, and were exiting him from the studio. When the smoke cleared, weeks later, our project was no longer viable since no one knew which end was up at the ship without the Master, Samuel Z. Arkoff, guiding it. Mike Selsman, Ralph Bakshi and I sat Shiva over the project.

Barbra Streisand shared a big estate with Jon Peters on Ramirez Canyon in Malibu. They called me one day all excited about the fact that a nearby Tudor mansion on three acres had become available. Wouldn't it be nice for us to become neighbors?

I went to see the property and was smitten. This was 1981, and the owner, Steve Rosen, insisted on $850,000 as the purchase price after much negotiation. I offered him $800,000 and he wouldn't budge. It was a strain, but I paid the final asking price, comfortable with the fact that the property value could go nowhere but up.

There were many improvements necessary to make the property ideal for my use. After the better part of a year, and the expenditure of more cash, I was able to dwell in my dream house. It boasted a cobble stoned courtyard, gated entrance, and had a two-story living room with windows floor to ceiling looking out upon two acres featuring a glorious English garden, complete with a stone-walled hot tub and a separate cottage, which had a secretary office plus room for three full-size automobiles. I located my office on the second level of the house, where I could view the front courtyard as well as the rear garden. The many-windowed Master bedroom suite had a 12x18 foot walk-in closet with a window, a sitting room with window seat and sofa, plus a custom, brick fireplace and French doors opening out to a lovely balcony. The huge his and hers master bath had a sunken tub and floor and walls of black marble.

The two-and-a-half acres and 150 specimen trees required constant watering and gardening. Jon and Barbra were helpful in having their gardening chief, Viviano (they had eight gardeners on a daily basis) lend me some help in taking care of the gardening requirements. I would see a lot of Viviano, because he came around every few days to make sure things were going well for me.

One day, Viviano showed up, looking quite furious. I invited him in for a drink to calm him down and asked if I could be of any help.

He said, "No, I can't talk about your friend."

I said, "Jon?"

He said, "Yes, he ordered me to do some work on another house he's building, and got me in trouble with Barbra when she found out."

"Well, you know Jon is very enthusiastic and impulsive and I'm sure he meant to tell her."

He continued, "Nothing of the kind. Jon has many secrets."

I said, "Well, he's pretty open with me."

Viviano said, "You're like all the rest of us. You want to believe the best."

My curiosity got the better of me and I asked, "What secrets is he withholding from me?"

He answered, "Last week we were riding along in the jeep on the Estate and he showed me a $50,000 check from Steve Rosen. Jon said to me, 'That's the way to make easy money,' as he folded the check up and put it in his pocket, 'That's my commission on the house sale to Jack Harris.'"

I immediately understood why Steve held out for the extra $50,000. It was Jon's secret commission on his sale of the house to me. I couldn't believe one of my best buddies for twelve years could do this to me. I was hurt beyond words and could only say, "Thanks for the information." My feelings for Jon were completely shattered. In the ensuing years he tried several times to do business with me on various films and I always rejected the idea.

One day in 1984, I was sitting in my home office, when I got a phone call from Chuck Russell, a production manager I had heard of but never met. He wanted to discuss remaking THE BLOB. He came out to Malibu and we had a luncheon meeting at the Sand Castle Restaurant while we watched bathers out the window near our booth. I listened carefully to his proposition.

He had a deal with a studio, but wouldn't name it. I told him to give me a few days and I'd get back to him.

Within hours, I had checked every studio and finally determined it was Embassy Pictures. I called Chuck and he laughingly said, "So, you figured out the studio."

I said, "Well, it's one of the things I know how to do – get to the bottom of whatever concerns my business."

We had a meeting with Bob Rheme at Embassy Pictures, and in ten minutes we made a deal for them to acquire an option to remake THE BLOB. Chuck Russell brought aboard his writing partner, Frank Darabont, who later would make his name famous by writing and directing THE SHAWSHANK REDEMPTION and developed the hit TV series *The Walking Dead* for AMC. It turned out that Frank was a classmate of my son at USC and had begged Anthony for over a year to introduce us. Anthony chose not to annoy me with stray introductions, but we met in this roundabout way anyhow. About a month later, Chuck, Frank and I had a story meeting to which I invited my son. They laid out an outline for their approach on THE BLOB remake.

I sat there in disbelief, since we had an early meeting in which I laid out a plan to take all the good stuff from the original movie and build upon it. They decided to go in a completely different direction.

I was shattered, since they had earlier asked me for a direction in plotting the new script. I proudly recited that the Blob is a mineral form of life from another world that gets here, consumes human flesh on contact, and grows at an alarming rate of speed. If not arrested or destroyed, it would envelop the earth. Our method of arresting was freezing done by locals without the necessity of calling in the Marines. The Blob was indestructible and not susceptible to poison, gas, fire and munitions. The Armed Forces and their artillery couldn't destroy The Blob. Chuck and Frank agreed to go back to the drawing board and get back to me within a month.

Two weeks went by and Chuck called me and told me he had an opportunity to direct the second sequel to A NIGHTMARE ON ELM STREET. I leapt at his opportunity because it could only be beneficial to my film to have him get his director stripes elsewhere first. The studio saw it my way, and he was off doing episode three of A NIGHTMARE ON ELM STREET 3: DREAM WARRIORS. The film has long been considered to be among the best in the long-running series, equal to if not better than the original. This turned out to be an excellent arrangement for all involved.

We were once again ready to start production, and the studio started delaying the start date. It soon became apparent that the studio was having the "shorts," or as they say in Hawaiian, "lacka money." We now were seeking another financing entity to back us.

Chuck's agent took him to Cannes for the film festival. They were able to strike a deal with Elliot Kastner and Andre Blay to independently finance THE BLOB remake. Of course they needed my approval to make the deal. I had been receiving phone calls from studios all over town asking me if I would bring the project to them. Jon Peters was one of the callers, and he offered me 100% of his position if I would do the picture through his company, Guber/Peters.

I told Jon I couldn't do it because he'd have all that work and no income from it and he would resent it.

He laughed and said, "You're making a mistake."

I wouldn't dream of doing the deal with him. I sat down with Elliot Kastner and Andre Blay. We renegotiated my agreement, and the deal was made.

We started pre-production in offices in the West Los Angeles area, and attacked the script again. When I strongly objected to the direction it was taking, Chuck told me to take it up with Andre Blay, who informed me that Chuck's contract gave him creative control. I was in a deal that I couldn't get out of and made up my mind to do lip service and nothing more for the production.

During the course of production, Blay and Kastner had made a deal with Columbia Pictures to distribute the final product, as they had been impressed with scenes that had been shown to them.

One evening after the picture was completed, we had a very private screening of the answer print, at Columbia Studio. My worst fears were realized. I felt the picture did not live up to the premise of the original film. When the lights went up, I looked around at the Columbia executives who were applauding what they had seen, and the CEO stood up and said to Blay and Kastner, "I hope you guys have sequel rights. This is a winner." It wasn't.

Ensconced in my Malibu manse, I dated occasionally and carefully. My pal, Mike Epstein, who owned a dating service, begged me to date one of his clients. Since she's a "private citizen" so to speak, and not in the public eye like some of the rest of these characters, we'll call her Erica. She was most attractive and anxious to leave her dead marriage for an eligible millionaire.

Erica was most amenable, but not attractive to me. We dated a few times and never hit the sack. One day at dusk, she showed up at my gate, explaining she was in the neighborhood and stopped by to take me to dinner if I was available. We went in her car to a nearby restaurant. Then she brought me home and we said a casual goodnight. While I was standing outside the car, the heavens opened up with a severe downpour of an electrical storm. She started crying and claimed an absolute fear of lightening and asked to stay a while until it let up. We watched TV while the storm raged unabated. After a couple of hours, she went out to her car and came back with a suitcase saying, "I might just spend the night with your permission."

I showed her to a guestroom and went to my bedroom. About one-half hour later, she entered my bedroom in a sexy black negligee. I was in bed and she unceremoniously jumped into the bed with me. "I'm determined to see if you can get it up," she announced. I asked her to please be on her way as soon as the storm stopped.

She left about 3:00 AM, much to my relief. Erica called me daily after that, but I was always "too busy" to see her. Eventually, I left her calls unanswered. But one day, I accidentally answered the phone and heard her voice. She had a proposal for me. If I would introduce her to a rich, gentleman friend, she would introduce me to her desirable, available girlfriend. To shut her up, I agreed. A month went by during which she would call to check weekly about our arrangement. One day I gave her telephone number to a horny friend, and she gave me the number for Judith Parker, owner of j.k. Parker & Associates, Inc., a successful and rapidly growing ad agency. Erica had a date with my friend that went nowhere. I never called Judith Parker, feeling that anyone worthy wouldn't have Erica for a friend. Erica inundated me with reminders to call Judith and agreed to stop calling me if I did. I called Judith's office and left word.

Weeks went by with no return call from Judith, and no more calls from Erica either. Eventually, Judith called me with apologies that Erica was overwhelming her with reminders to call me. We talked for about forty-five minutes. Judith was full of interesting, intelligent and appealing conversation. Judith now swears that she fell in love with me on the phone. We made a date to meet for dinner in Santa Monica at the Ivy at the Shore, a well-known watering hole and meeting place.

We pulled into the parking lot at the same time. I liked what I saw and apparently Judith wasn't turned off either. We spent almost two hours of the most pleasant time I can remember. I was astounded that Judith could turn out to be such an attractive, intelligent lady that I met through Erica. I fell in love with Judith. She was thirty years my junior, but our thoughts and ideas were as though we were contemporaries. I was thrilled at how quickly we became a couple. Our schedules didn't always allow togetherness. J.k. Parker & Associates had become one of the spear-headers of health advertising and marketing. I was in the middle of handling various dealings with THE BLOB remake during our courtship. We enjoyed and cherished the times we spent together.

We took a pre-Halloween weekend trip to New York. I proposed at Maxim's, a black tie restaurant. Judith gave me the shortest speech of her career, "Doesn't our age difference bother you?"

I answered, "Of course. You're the oldest gal I ever dated. But you're the love of my life. I'll just have to live with it."

Judith wanted some time to decide. Although that wasn't the answer I had hoped for, I gave her two weeks to think it over. Promptly at the end

Jack and Judith Harris wedding, December 19, 1987.

of two weeks, I took her to dinner at Splash in Malibu and got down on bended knee and proposed again. Judith said, "Yes", with familiar Malibu faces looking on and offering their congratulations.

We were married December 19, 1987. We had a full-blown wedding celebration, tented and orchestrated at the Malibu mansion. This was the first meaningful wedding celebration for me. It was my best decision ever. Having met just four months earlier, Judith remembers it as the only impulsive thing she had ever done in her life. I'm still amazed to think that it was marrying me. I'm a lucky man.

Of all the people that I've known, I've never found anybody that is crazier about the movies and more star struck and more passionate about the Academy Awards than Judith. I hadn't realized that until the first time we watched the Academy Awards together, a very brief time into our new marriage. We watched the ceremony on TV together as THE LAST EMPEROR dominated the evening, winning nine awards including Best Picture.

Judith requested we watch the show with a monk-like reverence, getting food before the show that was only to be eaten during commercial breaks (which was also the only time we were allowed to talk). I dressed up in a smoking jacket, with Judith wearing pajamas, a comfortable robe, and high heels. We had so much fun. But the following year, Judith begged me to take her to the Shrine Auditorium to attend the ceremony in the flesh.

Of course, I did. Judith still cites it as a highlight of her life. I had insisted that she get a fantastic dress for the Academy Awards. It was a very tight and slinky mermaid dress, fitting her stunning form. When we entered the auditorium, Judith said, "Please, whatever you do, don't leave me. I can't walk up or down the stairs without a little help."

Almost as soon as we had entered the auditorium, Judith turned around and I was gone. She saw me a few rows down, with Jack Lemmon and some other friends. She was embarrassed and stuck on the stairs. But a friendly woman saw her predicament and helped her to her seat. Judith spent the rest of the night watching the ceremony in awe.

Judith relishes Hollywood life and culture. Although my hearing loss (still, not bad for ninety-six) makes attending movies and screenings a challenge, we spend the fall and winter months catching up on DVDs of films in "Oscar contention" that get sent to members of the Academy. She hangs on every word of all of my Hollywood stories, which is a big part of why I'm writing this book. So she and my family, friends, and fans of cinema may enjoy them, as one of my contracts might say, "in perpetuity."

In 1988, Judith and I attended a packed house, sneak preview of THE BLOB remake in El Monte, CA. The preview cards reflected the audience's mildly entertained demeanor, but there was still the premiere in 2,000 theatres coming up.

On September 12, 1987, there was a showing of the original film at the Nuart Theatre in West L.A., whereby the soundtrack was turned off and the picture was voiced by a group of seven actors led by Kent Skov. Their troupe was called the L.A. Connection, and the aim of the new voicing was big laughs. Coincidentally, on our way to the L.A. Connection screening, Judith and I drove by the Bruin Theatre in Westwood and were tremendously disappointed to see no lines and spotty attendance at the world premiere of the remake of THE BLOB.

We went on to the Nuart with heavy hearts, which was soon lifted by the packed house waiting to see THE BLOB/L.A. Connection screening. THE BLOB remake bombed at the box office, making my co-producers happy that they had taken the huge advance from Columbia, leaving them with very little exposure. It took years of ancillary showings to get to a profit stage. The funny thing is, that when theatres and TV channels want to play THE BLOB, they pass on the remake and come to me for the original 1958 version.

In 1988 Judith, Kent Skov, and I sat in a meeting during which Kent was pitching putting the L.A. Connection version of THE BLOB on film, making it possible for us to show the performance in thousands of venues without transporting live actors and musicians. I had been considering it for a while and always had doubts.

I looked at the cost potential and figured we could get by very reasonably since all we had to do was put together a soundtrack, along with putting a mouth on the Blob itself at Judith's suggestion. It took well over $200,000 to finish BLOBERMOUTH and create a promotional campaign. The theme of the picture had the Blob and Steve McQueen as rival stand-up comics trying to get on "The Tonight Show." A mouth was animated on the existing footage of the Blob and worked very convincingly. Beside the painstaking animated mouth on the Blob, turning the movie THE BLOB into the movie BLOBERMOUTH was a herculean task involving many hours on the sound stage, closely synchronizing all of the new dialogue and music to the original film. It took a surprisingly lengthy time for recording, and the result was a hilarious take on this science fiction icon.

Judith alerted me to all of her skills she acquired during her production of over 3,000 commercials, and she was a priceless addition to our supervisory production staff, producing the music video segments and adding her voice to a couple of the characters. Voice Over talent was another one of the hats Judith wore as a former spokesperson for Sears for seven years in her previous incarnation.

Jack and Judith, present Blobermouth at New York Independent Film Festival in 1989.

Film festivals around the world became enamored by BLOBERMOUTH, and we traveled with it to Florence, Italy where it was exhibited in a 2,500 year old amphitheatre, which was quite a thrill in itself. We had a sellout crowd in Gothenburg, Sweden, who loved the idea of THE BLOB and BLOBERMOUTH on a double bill. The same thing happened in Taormina, Sicily, where again it was exhibited in a 2,000-year-old amphitheatre. In San Sebastian, Spain, we were toasted celebrities when the double feature BLOB show played there.

So far, we are still trying to recover the BLOBERMOUTH production costs after exercising television, VHS, and even DVD rights. Apparently, no one wants to laugh at THE BLOB.

One morning at the Florence Film Festival, we were summoned to the Palazzo de Congressi for a press interview and were ushered into a large meeting room, the walls of which were emblazoned with original Michelangelo murals. Judith and I were so fascinated with the artwork that a couple of times we had to have our attention brought back to the interviews at hand.

At a cocktail party later, I was congratulated by Dr. Fabrizio Fiumi, the festival director, for being one of the most astute producers he'd ever met. Speilberg and many other names raced through my mind as he was speaking. I asked him, "What is so remarkable about me?"

He said, "You have *The Blob Show* on RAI Network which beams all over Italy."

I said, "Well, I'm glad to hear about that. What's the show about?"

He looked at me quizzically, "Now, you're pulling my leg."

I was serious, "No, I truly never heard of *The Blob Show*."

He said, "Señor Harris, you lie with a straight face. Not only are you astute, you're very funny."

I calmed him down long enough to elicit from him the nature of *The Blob Show* which was broadcast every night at 7:30 PM on RAI 1, and it showed clips from THE BLOB mixed in with all the bloopers in the news from the day before.

We were glued to the TV set at 7:30 that night and saw the live daily segment of The Blob Show. That night it had something to do with footage of Steve McQueen going to the telephone and having it answered by an Italian hooker for an overheated exchange. Without boring the reader, I can sum up six months of negotiations with the RAI brass, which resulted in a $250,000 payment to us for copyright violation.

Early in 1994, I discovered that Good Times Video was illegally distributing home videos of THE BLOB. I notified them by letter and telephone of their copyright infringement. They rebuffed me with a perfunctory claim that my picture had no current copyright and was, indeed, in the public domain. Part of my claim was furnishing them with a currently valid copyright renewal. Good Times ignored me and continued to distribute THE BLOB videos.

Copyright experts Bishop/Barry was the law firm I enlisted to protect our rights. A minor officer of the firm was assigned to the case, but in short order, after spending a week with his part-time assistant, Steven M. Rubenstein, I determined that Steve was, indeed the guy, whose persistence and dedication would insure the validity of my claims.

After months of pre-trial testimony, actually on the eve of the Federal trial, Good Times anxiously and contritely contacted me with a settlement offer of $175,000. I couldn't have done it without Steve. He documented an invincible Chain-of-Title that was so perfect it led to the settlement, but it also left Steve disappointed that he didn't get to really beat them in a court of law.

Steve soon opened his own office, attracting worthy clients, and has successfully litigated a wide range of legal situations including representing the wife in the Rupert M. Murdoch divorce proceedings. Steve has helped me in numerous copyright violation actions as well as routine legal matters, including the friendly and pleasurable experience of Jay Leno using the footage on *The Tonight Show.* Steve and I have become good friends, and Judith and I value our relationship with Steve and his wife Sally.

⌘

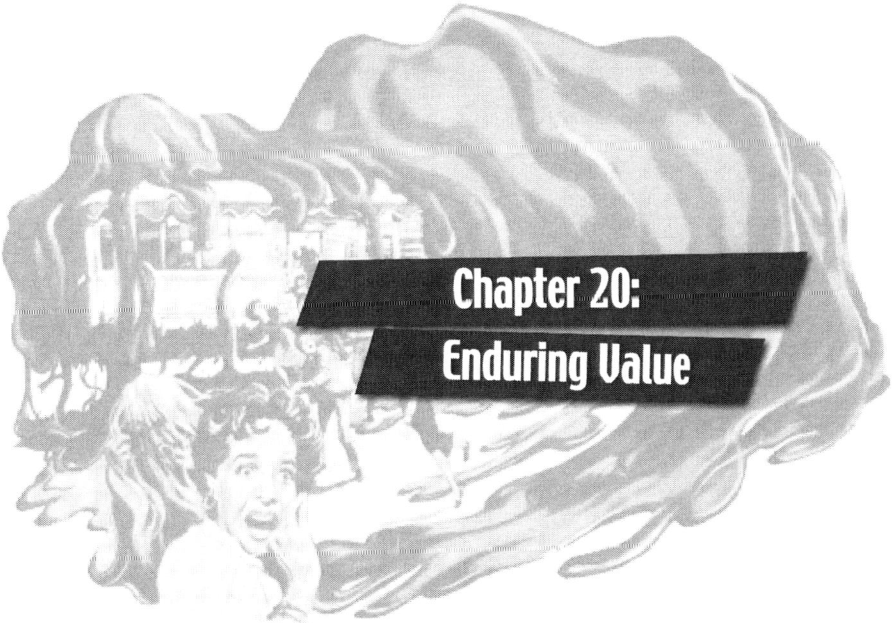

Chapter 20: Enduring Value

After being long out of contact, Jon Peters called me in early 2002 for a "reminiscing luncheon" at his recently acquired mansion near Beverly Hills. I graciously joined him and was told about how precious our friendship was to him. Having long since ended his romantic relationship with Barbra, he was solicitous and forthcoming about his new wife and daughter. I was effusive about my relationship with Judith. It was a joyful occasion.

A few weeks later, I was approached via email by Scott Rudin, who at the time had a first-look deal at Paramount Pictures, to do a new, scary, high-budget remake of THE BLOB. Since winning his Oscar in 2008 for NO COUNTRY FOR OLD MEN, Rudin has almost exclusively worked on "arthouse" projects with the likes of Tom Hanks, Meryl Streep, Aaron Sorkin, and the Coen brothers. Even though his career was already headed in that direction with THE HOURS for which Nicole Kidman won an Oscar, he was still making films for a more mainstream marketplace that included ZOOLANDER, SCHOOL OF ROCK, the remake of THE STEPFORD WIVES, and THE VILLAGE. He felt a remake of THE BLOB was canonical with those, and Paramount was a good home for the project. I told him the time was ripe. He put me in touch with Jeffrey Freidman of business affairs. Although it must be said that Rudin is one of the most talented men in the business, with the seemingly innumerable accolades to prove it, every legendary story you've heard about his temper is probably true and then some, as I would come to learn. Still, after a month of negotiations, we had what was, in my opinion, a viable deal.

I was agonizing over the Paramount deal when Judith suggested to me, "Why don't you call your old friend, Jon Peters, and get his advice? If anyone knows a good deal, it's him."

I called Jon. Before I could get the deal laid out to him, he started screaming at me, "Why the fuck should you make such a deal with that asshole? Give me two days! Do it with me, and I'll take it to Warner Brothers, and get you more front money and you can have half of my piece of the gross."

To my shocked amazement, I got a call the very next day from Sandra Smockler, the head of business affairs at Warner Brothers offering me the deal Jon had outlined, including my half share of his gross participation. I told her I would get back to her. Before I could hang up the phone, Jon Peters was on the other line yelling at my secretary to put me right on.

I picked up the phone and heard his litany of "Don't be a fuckin' idiot! This is a dream deal! Say Yes, now! We'll be in front of the camera for a 2003 release."

I called Scott Rudin and tried to gracefully decline his offer. His business affairs guy called me back to say that Paramount was examining their legal position. I said, "We don't have a contract. I'm allowed to reject an offer."

Within two months, the Warner Brothers deal was executed. They paid a substantial deposit versus millions on a two-year option to get a picture started.

For the first time in my life, I found out what development hell is really all about. Jon had a Kabbalah meeting at his home every Thursday night and invited Judith and me to join the group. At the first meeting we attended, Jon took the floor away from Kabbalah Rabbi Aton, with a special announcement, "I want you to meet my dear friend of thirty years, Jack H. Harris and his beautiful wife, Judith Parker Harris. Jack is my mishpucha (family). I just saved him from getting lost at Paramount with his most precious project, the remake of THE BLOB. He'll tell you that he's got a dream deal, both in front money as well as back end money, and part of the gross from the first dollar. I'm going to see to it that this picture gets made on a big budget and will make more noise at the box office than anything we can remember." He also explained that the Kabbalah teaches you to always make good on a promise, "I've owed Jack a favor for many years. Furthermore, this will give my good dear friend and mishpucha a wonderful guarantee of financial security in his later years."

In time, his promises proved to be meaningless. As the months wore on, I was so disgusted with Jon's inaction on my project that Judith had to drag me each week to the Kabbalah meetings so that he would see my face and be reminded that THE BLOB deal existed and needed to be acted upon. In addition to his loss of interest in our project, he also divorced himself from the Kaballah after a number of intense years of practice, during which he proclaimed what a changed man he became due to the Kabbalah and how much better his life was. All of this went down the tubes like a dose of salts when he got turned off. During the last face-to-face I had with Jon, I asked what caused the delay. He dismissed me with, "We just can't get a good 'take'."

At the end of eighteen months, I could no longer get Jon on the phone, and the project was languishing at Warner Brothers. Jon had one thing on his mind and it wasn't THE BLOB. He'd been trying for five years to get the new SUPERMAN made and during these past eighteen months, the picture had been green-lit and stopped twice. Two directors walked out on him, causing the stoplights to go on. During all this time,

Jon and I had stopped communicating and the studio was acting as intermediary, with little response from Jon's office.

With Jon's attention tied up in this mishegas, I contacted Bob Bissell, head of acquisitions at Warner Brothers. We arranged a meeting for us with his assistant, David Bierbauer, during which he enthusiastically expressed his excitement for THE BLOB remake. Bob came prepared with a list of six writers whom he believed were capable of delivering a good take on the picture. He also had trouble reaching Jon, even though they were two buildings away from each other. I read some of the preliminary work that some of the writers had done, and suggested that Joe Ballerini looked like he had the smarts to bring in a good screenplay.

Joe worked with me for a couple of sessions as I filled him in on the background of THE BLOB and the elements I thought should be brought to bear in the new script. He wrote a treatment that ultimately reached me for consideration. Bob was most enthusiastic. I said, "Let's go for a screenplay." Bob agreed.

A few weeks later, I called Bob one day and was told by David that he had checked himself into an emotional care facility. I asked where things were on the screenplay. He said, "All this happened within the last two days, and I'd have to dig in and see what's what."

I asked to see a copy of Joe Ballerini's screenplay and was told I'd have it in a few days.

I had reservations about the treatment, but assumed that these issues would be resolved in the screenplay. Just the opposite occurred. The issues were expanded and multiplied. It was a double disaster. If anyone is reading this who ever wants to be involved in development or production as the screenwriter writing a treatment for consideration for a gig please take a lesson from this story. Especially when trying to get jobs or when projects are going through development, loglines, pitches, outlines, and treatments all exist for a reason: That is so a producer or executive may know what they're getting when putting a writer on a project, and so everybody may be on the same page with problems, solutions, and what's expected. Never think that problems in an early outline or treatment will magically go away in a full screenplay. Have it figured out at an early stage. Any chink in the armor will only serve to bring down the entire suit you're trying to build.

I communicated my fears to David, who let me know that he had just heard that Bob had just been permanently ensconced at the hospital with a complete, mental breakdown. At that point, the only classy thing to do is to say that you wish the man well and then go about your other business.

There were suddenly only two months to go before the expiration of Warner Brothers' two-year option. I called David to get an update. He bitterly complained to me about the killing pressure of his schedule and time constraints. I asked him why he didn't take a walk. He said to me, "Jack, you're a witch. I just accepted a deal from Dreamworks this morning."

There went my Warner Brothers connection. The next week, it was announced that someone had been brought over from Disney to take Bob Bissel's job. He and I discussed THE BLOB remake project and he said, "I have to figure out whether we should make this picture right away or ever."

I diplomatically ended the conversation. I had decided to just let the clock tick for the seven-and-a-half weeks remaining on the deal. I hoped that Warner Brothers would not call me.

Two days after the expiration date, I called Warner Brothers' head of business affairs, Sandra Smockler, and she told me how unhappy she was that the deal had not gone forward. I thanked her for her concerns and told her I had confidence I'd be able to set up the picture elsewhere. On June 16th, 2005, the project was free again.

I had been working with Brian Witten, Vice President of Paramount, on a deal to remake 4D MAN. On June 30th, 2005, Brian called me to tell me that Paramount wasn't interested in the 4D MAN deal, but if the rights to THE BLOB were ever available again, they wanted me to know they'd be ready to make a deal. I said, "Have your business affairs guy call me. The rights are now available."

The agreement took mere days to complete and on March 27th, 2005, Paramount paid me a substantial deposit versus millions on a two-year option fee for remaking THE BLOB, with Scott Rudin as my partner. Scott Aversano, Rudin's assistant, was in constant touch with me. We discussed all avenues of getting underway on a screenplay. Then early in May, I read in the trades that Scott Rudin had accepted a deal from Disney to be a supplier to Miramax Pictures and their other affiliates. This was in direct response to Disney having lost Harvey and Bob Weinstein in their settlement of the Miramax Pictures dissolution.

Now, Scott Rudin was off the Paramount lot, but THE BLOB deal was still working. Paramount CEO, Sherry Lansing, a big fan of THE BLOB, exited the company six weeks later. Then her top assistants, including Brian Witten, were replaced one-by-one. Gail Berman, another BLOB lover, became the new head of production, but was replaced in March of 2007. Sometimes you have to wonder if there's another industry in which people change employers about as often as they change their socks, but I digress.

After eighteen months of development, the rough draft screenplay of THE BLOB remake was presented to me. Although I was thrilled that it happened, I drew up a short list of suggested corrections, which were accepted positively by Scott Rudin. The present option was set to expire March 16th, 2007, so the rough draft screenplay was submitted for a green light. Scott Rudin was told by the new people in charge that they had no time to read the screenplay, but THE BLOB remake was not the kind of film they cared to produce.

Scott Rudin requested a thirty-day free option to see if he could replace Paramount. I rejected the proposal.

He emailed back, "You've got to be kidding me."

That was our last email contact, which reminded me that over the years of our attempt to work together, all of my contacts with Scott Rudin were limited to email. He would have his assistant get me on the phone, then I was told to wait, then I'd hear, "Mr. Rudin has to take another call, but will contact you via email." Over time, I did have telephone conversations with several of his assistants, but I never talked directly with Scott Rudin.

One day, Judith answered the phone and it was Scott Rudin, via his assistant. She was so excited, because at last it looked like we would connect. I was on another line, so Judith told them to please hold and that I'd be with them in seconds. The assistant quickly replied, "Oh no, Mr. Rudin does not want Mr. Harris to interrupt himself, we'll contact him by email." The assistant hung up before he could hear Judith's protestations of, "No, no, Mr. Harris wants to be interrupted for Mr. Rudin. He wants to speak to Mr. Rudin…" The line was dead and we were back to email. We were also back to THE BLOB remake languishing for a period of time.

I've been told not to take it personally, that Scott Rudin hardly ever speaks by telephone with anyone.

⌘

Chapter 21: Blobfest

Back in 1957, during the production of THE BLOB, we needed a theatre location to support the now iconic movie theatre sequence. The nearest theatre to Chester Springs was about five miles away. It was The Colonial Theatre in Phoenixville, Pennsylvania.

The theatre was built in 1903 and supported live entertainment as well as silent short movies. After entering the "sound movies" era and still sustaining live performances, The Colonial survived a series of ownerships and remodels to reach the tired status of a small town film house. It was this shabby setting that was faithfully photographed during the production. I had negotiated with theatre owner, Norman Silverman, the sum of $75 to shoot there for three days. He cussed me out for being so cheap. I told him we were immortalizing his dump. Truer words have never been spoken. As the years went by, the theatre went downhill and eventually closed in 1991.

In 1999, I got a phone call from a lady named Mary Foote, who explained she was the managing director of the now reopened, and almost refurbished by local investors, Colonial Theatre in Phoenixville, Pennsylvania. I wished her success and if I could help to let me know.

It was strange to suddenly get a phone call from that theater in Pennsylvania after so many years.

She said, "I appreciate your kind wishes. I called you to discuss something with you." She explained that her non-profit group had come up with an idea to stimulate attendance by running THE BLOB in our theatre and calling it a "Blobfest," in order to use the profits to help complete the remodeling of the theatre.

I responded positively, and told her I'd make a print available for the occasion. She thanked me profusely and set a date upon which she would need the print. I never thought of asking for a film rental because it was a non-profit event for a good cause.

This simple Blobfest notion turned into a standing-room only attraction and an enormous box office hit for the Colonial Theatre. The theatre people decided that the next year they would repeat the same idea, up the admission price, and run the Blobfest for two days. For the next year's Blobfest a new deal was drawn. In addition to transportation costs, the Colonial Theatre would have to pay a token rental charge for the use of the print. Mary Foote agreed.

As the years progressed, this annual event, the middle Friday and Saturday of each July, kept growing in importance for the theatre. The extra charge for ticket cost kept multiplying. About four years ago, the film rental rose substantially per showing.

They sent me publicity telling about what went on at Blobfest, including parades, costume contests, unique t-shirts, street vendors, restaurants with specials on BLOB-wiches, a giant BLOB cut-out with holes in it as a photo op for interested patrons at $20.00 each, a live re-enactment of the "run from the theatre" scene, plus appearances by cast and crew of the original production.

Mary Foote kept asking me to come and take a bow at the Blobfest, but a round-trip to Phoenixville, Pennsylvania was not on my schedule. Mary told me in January, 2007 that it would be a good time for me to show up. It was the 50th Anniversary of THE BLOB.

I told her THE BLOB was released in 1958. She reminded me that the production of THE BLOB was completed in 1957. Therefore, it's the 50th anniversary of the completion of THE BLOB.

I kept arguing with myself that I had to find time for this event. I had so many other profitable things to look after, that this seemed like a no contest against my showing up.

In early June of 2007, after discussing the matter with Judith, ad infinitum, she claimed, "It is the 50th Anniversary and it would be a good idea if we went." She convinced me. There was only one complication, the National Speakers Association of the Greater Los Angeles Area chapter, of which she was President, had their annual convention the four days preceding the time we were due to be in Phoenixville on July 13th. We compromised, and left L.A. for Philadelphia early on the morning of July 13th. We arrived in Philadelphia at about 8:00 PM, even though Judith only arrived home hours before our take off.

We had set up our arrival at Phoenixville to take place for the second day, July 14th at 11:00 AM. It was also a chance to spend a few hours with my grandson, Jonathan Sinay, who was at school in nearby New Jersey.

We arrived promptly on July 14th and found Phoenixville to be completely "Blobbed". Every storefront, every structure, had evidence of the Blob from huge red balloons to fluffy bed comforters to a three story Blob structure above the marquee of the theatre. All of the things described earlier were magnified immensely in person.

We took some pictures and stopped by the theatre for a few minutes. We went to have lunch across the street where I was waylaid by a reporter for the *Philadelphia Inquirer.* I gave him an interview as I stood next to our dining table awaiting the food we had ordered. This interview was printed in the Sunday *Inquirer,* July 15th Edition with true facts and numerous color illustrations of the doings.

My next chore was to attend the Q&A discussion on the stage of the theatre. With great fanfare, I was presented with the center seat on the dais. I was introduced to the audience with great applause, which I acknowledged with thanks. Then the interviews started on my right.

First up was Wes Shank, whose claim to fame was that he purchased the leftover Blob piece of silicone used in the movie and still in its original container, a five-gallon metal drum. He took this as an appointment to perpetuate the history of the Blob – even though he didn't have a damn thing to do with it. Shank had conducted tours of the studio where THE BLOB was produced and sold autographed pictures of himself holding the Blob can. He announced that he was now writing the history of the Blob – a book to be published in 2008. It hasn't happened yet.

I sat quietly aghast.

The next person to be introduced was a little, old lady limping on the stage with a crutch. Her connection was that she fell down and broke her leg in the theatre running scene. She was duly modest but truly hurt during shooting.

Next up was Kate Phillips, who told about her connection with the screenplay as though she had written it. She was making it sound like the real originator of the piece, Ted Simonson had merely assisted her, she claimed. Ted originated, executed, and should be solely credited as writer of THE BLOB screenplay. Rody Nelson, who assisted Ted, deserves credit for the key closing line, "As long as the arctic stays cold."

I was there when the script was written. I never met her. She was the woman brought in to sweeten up Ted Simonson's script due to the momentary insecurity of Shorty the director, only to be immediately fired after insulting his wife, Jean. She went on to explain how she named The Blob, this aroused my interest, since I had named The Blob myself.

She said she was finishing the script, and she made her husband read it. He said to her, "Kate, this is a Blob of a monster."

She said, "That's it, we'll call it THE BLOB."

She announced that the next day would be her 95th birthday and I felt that dementia had set in as the only excuse for her speech.

Kate Phillips passed away in 2008. Her obituary emphasizing her lies caused me to dig up her contract, which shows that she verified receipt of payment in full with no mention of the ongoing percentage she claimed in the agreement. Her IMDB and Wikipedia pages (invariably sources of trustworthy information) give her credit she doesn't deserve. An IMDB "bio," written by someone who likely has an axe to grind, takes the deal she made with us and inaccurately paints it in a negative light. Hopefully, the release of this book will help correct some of these movie history distortions.

I was next up and gave my usual scintillating performance, and the audience responded warmly. They didn't know that I had bitten my tongue and held my true comments about what was going on.

The other celebrity was Kris Yeaworth, Shorty's son, who was nine-years-old at the time of the production. He could only add hearsay to the proceedings.

The last celebrity was a stranger to me, whose claim to fame was he was the clack boy on the picture. He had outtakes of almost every scene where he clacked the board to the director's order of "action." At least he did have something to do with the making of the picture, although a very minor part.

I signed autographs for about two-and-a-half hours and got an idea about how many posters were sold at $10 each so they could be embellished with my signature.

There was a farewell dinner where all the "celebrities" again showed up, and I had to listen to more malarky from Kate Phillips. She asked if I would be present at the next Blobfest and I diplomatically said, "I'll see." The positives I took from the whole experience were the unprecedented cooperation and outstanding support of the entire town of Phoenixville, from the emblazoned shop windows, costume contests, and parades, and that THE BLOB has an ongoing iconic effect upon theatre audiences near and far, young and old, who make it an annual pilgrimage to Blobfest. All of it very pleasing to my heart.

Every year, I make sure Blobfest has a very carefully cared for film print. They could use DVDs, but they have the original film. It's kept in a vault, treated, and delivered once a year to the theater. Fortunately, the same people remain in charge and are very friendly.

One person was missing from the proceedings, Shorty. As I sat there, my mind was drawn with thunderous clarity to July 20th, 2004. I received a chilling telephone call from dear friend Jean Yeaworth, telling me that her husband, Shorty, was killed in a road accident while supervising the construction of a theme park called, "The Jordanian Experience At Aquaba Gateway" in Jordan.

I had taken Shorty away from his first love, religious films in 1956 with the production of THE BLOB. The experience taught me what a talented filmmaker and good friend Shorty was to be associated with. We became a perfect team and continued together on 4D MAN, and our final movie together, DINOSAURUS. Reluctantly, I watched Shorty go back to making religious films with Billy Graham. I couldn't understand his leaving our industry since being in it was the culmination of my ambitions, but I respected his religious calling. In 1967, he had completed a film he couldn't place in theatres. I promptly donned my distributor cap to launch his production of WAY OUT in the Loews Theatre circuit in New York, creating a pattern that he and his company were able to follow. We continued our contact through the years and I always looked forward to his trips to the West Coast. Shorty's passing left an unfillable void in my life. We often argued passionately about aspects of the films we were making. It's easy to see that as water under the bridge when you can look back and realize it was all out of love for the films and ultimately to their benefit. Jean and Kris are the biggest fans of THE BLOB, and still have all of Shorty's original mementos from the film. I'm happy to say that we're still friends and we still keep in touch.

Years ago, Peter Becker of Criterion Productions distributed THE BLOB and a special DVD version of EQUINOX in all foreign territories. This package was very successful, Peter just renewed the contract with a hefty advance payment.

It was indeed a thrill to sit down with Jack Woods again for a couple of hours as we reminisced on recording our adventures during the production of EQUINOX. On July 12, 2006, the famed Egyptian Theatre in Hollywood was the site of a special evening devoted to the showing of EQUINOX and in person were Dennis Muren, Jack Woods, Forrest Ackerman and myself plus the cast and crew of the picture. We all made speeches and signed autographs until midnight. The sale of the two-disc DVD package with many "extras" began with a loud bang to golden revenues. The physical distributor, Bruce Vanezzia of Image Entertainment, swears that it will outgross THE BLOB DVD domestically.

On June 2, 2007, I got a phone call from Roy Lee, head of a Dimension Picture subsidiary, to discuss the availability of THE BLOB for remake. The next day, Judith and I met with Roy Lee, Richard Saperstein, and Brian Witten, former VP of Paramount, (whom I failed to recognize, because since his Paramount days he lost fourty pounds). We had an entirely positive meeting. One hour after returning to my office, I had a call from business affairs head, Arthur Kaufman, to discuss a deal with Dimension to acquire the remake rights. Within hours, I was negotiating with Arthur Kaufman and his assistant, Andrew Kramer, until we reached a deal in principle.

Things were moving so fast. I almost missed the fact that Brian Witten associate of Roy Lee had lit a fire under Dimension that started it all. The main points of the very rich deal were mutually agreeable, and I appointed my legal rep, Steve M. Rubenstein, to iron out the final agreement fine points. After three weeks of back and forth, we hit a snag. Dimension wanted a limitless term in which to make a sequel and I insisted on a three-year limitation for tying up my rights. Sad to say, I could not agree to their request, so we parted amicably. It seemed like a good marriage, but I couldn't enter into a possible forever tie-up of THE BLOB rights.

⌘

Chapter 22: Film Library

I have about twelve titles in the DVD market and the most outstanding financial returns have been for THE BLOB. Through the years since THE BLOB was made, it developed another revenue source for me in the form of film clips. There was a private bank in Pittsburgh that was up against the monolithic, multi-branch banks. They used The Blob to represent that menace of big, multi-branch, impersonal banks. The Blob ate up small banks, but not this one. It came to the rescue with personal service and care that can only be offered by a private bank. There was a San Francisco automotive repair shop that created a TV spot to show that it could correct wrongs done to your automobile by shady Blob shops.

By far the best use of clips was by Jay Leno and his writers. Jay usually announced a primo performance of a famous entertainer and claims that he had surveillance cameras in attendance at the performance. Then he ran THE BLOB clip showing people running and screaming out of THE BLOB infested theatre, with the marquee advertising the performer Jay was named. The clip ends with the Police Chief cocking his rifle and saying, "That's the worst thing I've ever seen." Jay had used this clip about ten times in the last three years of his show.

In 2008, I granted permission to Heal the Bay to use a parody poster calling attention to "The Storm Drain Blob." 2000 posters were distributed in California. In 2009, ABC secured a Blob clip and an original Blob poster to use in one of their segments of *Criminal Minds.*

My film library continues to be attractive to the industry as well as returning audiences and new fans. Eighteen of my titles are in various stages of theatrical, television, and DVD distribution. As various agreements mature, they are either renewed or placed with new distribution houses. Under current discussion are deals to remake 4D MAN, DINOSAURUS and EQUINOX. I trust that it is merely a matter of time before these projects will find their way into actual production.

The entertainment industry has and continues to be a marvelous source of joy and success for me. In 1952, I predicted that television would become the main source of entertainment and information to the masses. Further, I incorrectly predicted the ultimate demise of movie-going. Movie theatres very much continue to serve mass audiences, in spite of drive-ins becoming almost non-existent. This is due in part to the stadium seating and multiple screen structures that now prevail. Theatres now range from ninety-seat, parlor-sized rooms, to huge elaborate spaces seating 600 or more viewers. Movie theatre attendance has gone from a habit to an intermittent visit, depending on patron word-of mouth-and want-to-see. Movie theatre grosses are still a substantial part of the economy, driven by the "tentpole" blockbusters.

It is a remarkable thing, when I think about it. To have lived through silent movies, shown en masse for a nickel, to digital distribution and immersive, 3D filmgoing experiences. In an attempt to build audiences, theaters are offering everything from gourmet meals to "4D" showings featuring motion seats and in-house special effects. Much like the innovations of the past, it will be fascinating to see which of these survive. Has anyone been to a theater and seen a great movie in gripping smell-o-vision lately?

Regardless of what delivery method is created in the future (VHS, DVD, internet), content will always be key. From the beginning of time, everyone has loved a visually presented story. As long as interesting stories are created, there will be an audience.

THE BLOB original enjoys constant television, DVD, and meaningful theatrical exposure. Its film clips remain in high demand. My dream has come true; the sequel is becoming a major movie gracing the marquees of leading theatres throughout the world. Producers Brian Witten and Richard Saperstein brought Simon West on board to direct. A live stage musical is also being written. In addition, there's a deal in the winds with a Canadian company on a sequel or remake of 4D MAN.

At ninety-six, with incredible success and nothing to prove, I work on these projects only because I love it. In addition to how deeply and dearly I love my wife, getting to do this work I love so much every day has helped keep me in such remarkable mental and physical health.

Our beloved country is presently recovering from a recession that is reminiscent of the Great Depression, which endowed the movie business with steady revenues in spite of 25% unemployment and other survival woes. Despite seasonal and yearly ebbs and flows, today theatres remain booming. They are still among the least expensive ways to escape life's trials.

I remain sincerely grateful for the providence that enabled me to spend eighty years in the developing motion picture business. I cherish the fates that afforded me the opportunity to be part of this wonderful industry. I've been honored to be an observer, theatre manager, publicist, distributor, producer, and director of movies.

The Motion Picture Academy has graced me by archiving my film library, my life's work. There have been numerous ups and downs, yet I consider myself blessed to have been a participant from the silent days to the 3-D, CG, I-MAXed world beaters of today.

Jack's entire family gathered when he received his star on the Hollywood Walk of Fame, February 4, 2014.

One of the biggest thrills in my life was getting my star on the Hollywood Walk of Fame. It started when I got a call from somebody I didn't know. I usually let Judith handle those calls. She took this on, and worked on it for about three years. Getting a star on the Walk of Fame is an incredibly long and involved process, of which I won't bore you with the details here. Another one of the greatest honors in my career was when I was awarded membership to the prestigious Academy of Motion Picture Arts & Sciences and my application was signed by the late Stanley Kramer. If you ask any cinema expert who the most influential producers in the history of movies are, there's a canonized list that includes (though not exclusively) Cecil B. DeMille, David O. Selznick, Irving Thalberg, Darryl Zanuck, and Stanley Kramer. Kramer earned nine Oscar nominations and won the Thalberg Award, for making remarkable films with a unique consciousness such as HIGH NOON, JUDGMENT AT NUREMBERG, and GUESS WHO'S COMING TO DINNER. He's so singularly important that he's one of the only

Jack and Judith sharing a "star" moment.

producers for whom our Guild has designated an award named in his honor. Regardless of how much professional success one has otherwise gained, by his signing his name to my legacy in this way was a deeply moving and humbling experience. I believe this greatly enhanced my prospects for earning my star.

It was a great surprise to me when Judith pulled me into her office to watch the live streaming of the event, during which those individuals who were getting stars the following year were to be announced. I sat down at her computer, but was cranky about it as I had other things to do. I realized it was the Hollywood Walk of Fame. The third name announced was mine. We both had tears in our eyes.

Many times during my career, I yearned that the path to production could be as accessible as if I were the offspring of an established producer, a la the Zanuck brood. However, in retrospect, I am grateful for the experience of having to get there the hard way through exhibition, distribution, promotion and finally, production.

Through the years, viewers have interpreted hidden messages and symbolism in THE BLOB. Many saw it as the need to stop communism from overtaking the world, others as the vile effect of monopolies gobbling up independent enterprise, still others saw THE BLOB as God's messenger sent to destroy the world's evil-doers.

In reality, THE BLOB was conceived only to do what good movies do best: entertain, stimulate good word-of-mouth, and maybe cause audiences to enjoy a scary moment or two.

THE BLOB is about having a good time at the movies.

Remember where you were the first time you saw THE BLOB?

⌘

Epilogue

In 2002, during our annual visit to my daughter Lynda and son-in-law Stewart's Little Lake Lodge in Aspen, Colorado, Judith was bemoaning the fact that we'd be leaving in two days. "Shame you haven't toured the mountain peaks," said Stewart. Judith expressed interest and Stewart got on the phone and reserved a jeep and guide for our next day. This house is at 8,000 feet, and the peaks are at 13,000 feet, a true thrill ride.

The next day, Judith and I plus our beloved grandson, Jonathan, bundled up to take the rail car to the top of the mountain to meet our guide. We entered the jeep and soon left the smooth road for the bumpy mountain peaks. Unfortunately, the jeep had no springs. We had ended up on a one-hour shake-up, the end of which couldn't come soon enough.

The reverse train ride to the town seemed bumpier than I remembered. Judith, Jonathan and I were thrilled to get to the house on solid ground. I felt strange but said nothing.

Next morning, we said bye-bye and headed for the airport. Checked in and settled in the waiting area, we heard the flight announced. I needed help to get up out of the chair I was sitting in. Safely on the plane, I turned on my TV and noticed it moving around, then swiftly so. I became nauseous and fell back in the seat. Judith called for assistance and two doctors came to the rescue. She then called our doctor in L.A.

Unable to walk, I was pushed to the car in a wheelchair and went directly to the hospital. One week in the hospital and I was diagnosed with Meniere's disease. I regained my balance and vision, but my hearing was permanently and dramatically affected.

Every remedial process was tried to correct my hearing loss and at the end of two years, acupuncture was added. It proved successful, and the episodes became less frequent. I turned to other creative methods to ward off episodes and then added other medicines to stop them.

I was once again fortunate that both my daughter and wife are natural healers. Judith had been able to overcome the ravages of Multiple Sclerosis, through the help of homeopathic treatments, and her own system of dealing with emotional blocks that can manifest in disease. She has dedicated her life to helping others identify blocks before they are knocked out by them. She calls her system Moving from Blocked to BlockBuster.

Lynda received her honorary doctorate from Bard College, making official what we already knew, that she is brilliant. She reads everything and stays on top of medical issues, always on the ready to care for family and friends.

I've had Judith coach me and watch my every step, and Lynda has sent over one miracle worker after another to get me back on my feet. Truly, their diagnoses are often right on.

We also can't overlook the power of loving and being loved.

After about three years, the episodes stopped and I was able to regain much of my balance. Sadly, after seven years, it came back as suddenly as it had ended. Vertigo would overtake me and the episodes would take control. I tried acupuncture again. This time it only seemed to make things worse.

Once again, our life was shoved into reverse. We couldn't go anywhere or see anyone without an episode coming on. Our active travel agenda was halted. Our focus was on healing again.

Eventually, the medication and my perseverance prevailed. Now my episodes are at least eight months apart.

My hearing depends on strong hearing aids, as I retain only 12% comprehension of words in each ear. My balance requires a walker or cane to walk, plus Judith's constant vigilance, as the episodes can come on quite suddenly. Each day I take a short nap after breakfast, and awake to a routine of push-ups, weight swinging, and a session on my bike exerciser. Then it's off to the shower and dress for lunch.

My business schedule varies daily. I have a half-hour outdoor walk, then another forty-five-minute nap. There's more time devoted to work, and then dinner, after which we gratefully watch TV shows in bed.

I still awake every morning with joy in my heart and gratitude for my family and my life in show business. Its a wonderful dream come true. I'm enjoying the hell outta my life and wish my readers similar benefits from your pursuits.

⌘

Author's Page

Jack H. Harris has been involved in some aspect of the film industry for almost ninety years. After stints as a child actor in Vaudeville and short films, Jack began working for his Father as a film projectionist at the age of fifteen. This began Jack's decades-long career in numerous aspects of film exhibition, distribution, and production.

Jack spent the early years of life and career in Philadelphia, standing out in the ranks of his industry with innovative promotions and distribution campaigns for films made by talents including Cecil B. DeMille and Laurel and Hardy. His career was put on hold to serve in World War Two, where Jack also stood out in the troops, rising from private to the rank of First Lieutenant.

Jack then spent many successful decades producing an iconic slate of films including 4D MAN, DINOSAURUS, UNKISSED BRIDE, EYES OF LAURA MARS, and most notably THE BLOB. Along the way, Jack discovered and mentored a group of A-list Hollywood talents including Steve McQueen, Patty Duke, John Landis, John Carpenter and Ivan Reitman.

Recently, a deal was concluded licensing Bally's (gaming devices) to manufacture BLOB emblazoned slot machines. Ultimately, hundreds will be placed in domestic and foreign casinos.

Jack remains active in managing his library and producing new films. He has two children, six grandchildren and four great-grandchildren. He lives in Beverly Hills with his wife Judith and their terrier mix rescue dog Jasper, twenty pounds of barking terror, but a real beauty.

PUBLISHED BY TVGUESTPERT PUBLISHING
(Previously Jacquie Jordan Inc. Publishing)

New York Times Bestselling
Author, CHRISTY WHITMAN
The Art of Having It All: A Woman's Guide to Unlimited Abundance
Paperback: $16.95
Nook/Kindle: $9.99
Audible Book: Coming Soon

EVE MICHAELS
Dress Code: Ending Fashion Anarchy
Paperback: $15.95
Kindle/Nook: $9.99
Audible Book: $17.95

DARREN CAMPO
Alex Detail's Revolution
Paperback: $9.95
Hardcover: $22.95
Kindle: $9.15

DARREN CAMPO
Alex Detail's Rebellion
Hardcover: $22.95
Kindle: $9.99

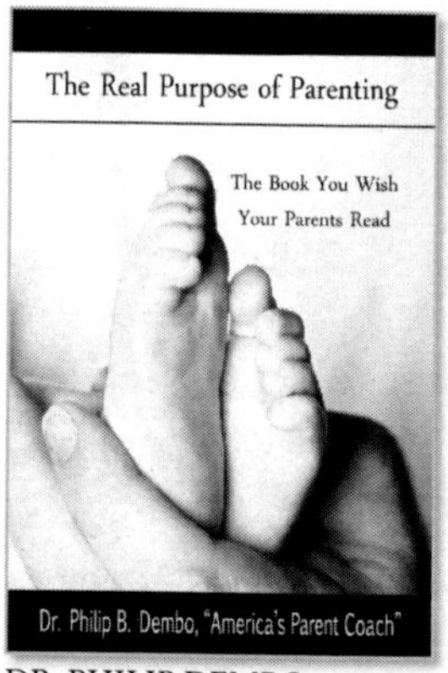

DR. PHILIP DEMBO
The Real Purpose of Parenting: The Book You Wish Your Parents Read
Paperback: $15.95
Kindle/Nook: $9.99
Audible Book: $23.95

TVGuestpert Publishing
11664 National Blvd, #345
Los Angeles, CA. 90064
310-584-1504
www.TVGPublishing.com

CHELSEA KROST
Nineteen: A Reflection of My Teenage Experience in an Extraordinary Life: What I Have Learned, and What I Have to Share
Paperback: $15.95
Kindle: $9.99
Audible Book: $14.95

JACQUIE JORDAN
Heartfelt Marketing: Allowing the Universe to be Your Business Partner
Paperback: $15.95
Kindle: $9.99
Audible Book: $9.95

DR. JEFF SCHWEITZER
The New Moral Code
Hardcover: $22.95
Audible Book: $17.95

JACQUIE JORDAN
Get on TV! The Insider's Guide to Pitching the Producers and Promoting Yourself
Published by Sourcebooks
Paperback: $14.95
Kindle: $9.99 Nook: $14.95

DR. JEFF SCHWEITZER
Beyond Cosmic Dice: Moral Life in a Random World
Hardcover: $22.95
Kindle: $9.99